Wildflowers of
Unalaska Island

Suzi Golodoff

Wildflowers of Unalaska Island

*A Guide to the Flowering Plants
of an Aleutian Island*

University of Alaska Press
Fairbanks, Alaska

© 2003 University of Alaska Press
        Box 756240-UAF
        Fairbanks, AK 99775-6240
        fypress@uaf.edu
        www.alaska.edu/uapress
All rights reserved.

2nd edition © 2013 University of Alaska Press
978-1-60223-220-4

The Library of Congress cataloged the previous edition as:
Golodoff, Suzi.
Wildflowers of Unalaska Island : a guide to the flowering plants of an
Aleutian island / Suzi Golodoff.
     p. cm.
Includes bibliographical references and indexes.
ISBN 1-889963-18-6
1. Wild flowers—Alaska—Unalaska Island—Identification. 2. Wild
flowers—Alaska—Unalaska Island—Pictorial works. I. Title.
QK146 .G66 2003
582.13'097984—dc21
                          2001027293

This publication was printed on acid-free paper that meets the minimum
requirements for the American National Standard for Information Science—
Permanence of Paper for Printed Library Materials ANSI Z39.48-1984.

Book design by Cameron Poulter.

All photographs and drawings are by Suzi Golodoff, except for those on page
46 of the least willow. The photo was taken by George Argus, and the drawing
is courtesy of the U.S. Forest Service.

Printed in China

For my mother and father,
who taught me a love of nature.

Armeria maritima *(Mill.) Willd. Thrift. Leadwort family. Found on sea cliffs and at high elevations.*

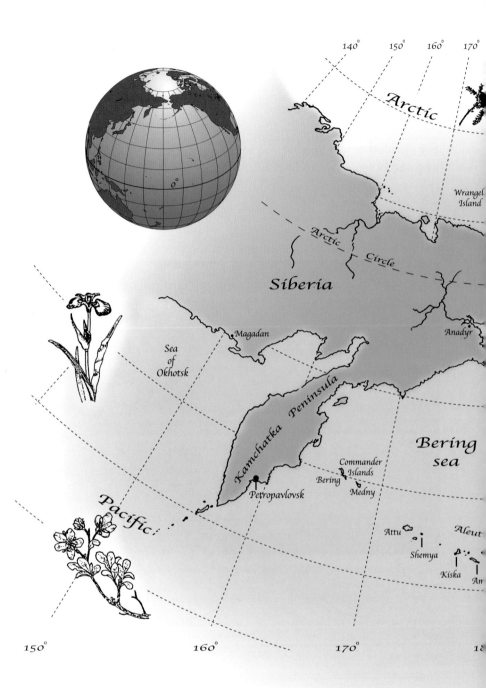

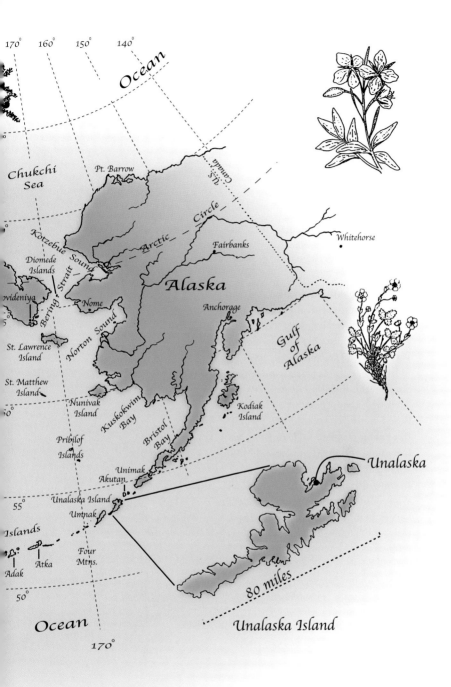

170° 160° 150° 140°

Ocean

Chukchi
Sea

Pt. Barrow

U.S.
Canada

Arctic *Circle*

Kotzebue Sound

Diomede
Islands

ovideniya

Bering Strait

Nome

Norton Sound

Fairbanks

• Whitehorse

Alaska

Anchorage

Gulf
of
Alaska

St. Lawrence
Island

St. Matthew
Island

Nunivak
Island

Kuskokwim Bay

Bristol Bay

Kodiak
Island

Pribilof
Islands

Unimak

Akutan

Unalaska Island

Umnak

Islands

Atka

Adak

Four
Mtns.

Unalaska

55°

50°

Ocean

170°

80 miles

Unalaska Island

Contents

ix

Contents

Cypripedium gutattum *SW., Lady's Slipper Orchid*

Acknowledgements

You hold this book in your hands only through the generosity and patience of others. My exceptional good fortune was having one of Alaska's finest botanists, Carolyn Parker, with the University of Alaska Museum of the North Herbarium at Fairbanks, as my friend and mentor throughout the project. She gave my work thorough review, answered countless questions, and without her, truly, this book would not exist. George Argus, botany collection manager at the Canadian Museum of Nature in Ottowa, kindly assisted with revising the willow section. Jerah Chadwick, former professor with the University of Alaska Interior-Aleutians Campus, gave much-needed editing advice along with a steady source of good humor. Generous editing help was also given by Philomena Hausler, Rick Knecht, Michael Krauss, Daniel H. Mann, Tom McKenna, and Teri Viereck. Early drafts required a steep learning curve with computers and Cheri Lee, former teacher at Unalaska City School, led the way. Jim and Shawn Dickson and the folks at City Hall also encouraged the book's beginnings.

   In gathering ethnobotanical information, I am indebted to the work that began in the early 1970s in the Unalaska City School, when elders from Unalaska and the surrounding villages of Atka, Nikolski, and Akutan were invited to share their traditional knowledge with students. Most of these elders are gone now, and the knowledge they shared with us would have been lost otherwise. Through the dedicated work of Ray Hudson, writer, historian and longtime teacher at Unalaska, and that of Father Ishmael and Mother Platonida Gromoff, much information on local plants was preserved, translated, and published for use in the Aleut Cultural Programs. Moses Dirks, who has taught Unangan language and culture for many years, encouraged my work and kindly accepted the task of going over the spellings. Nick Galaktianoff, Sr., elder and storyteller, generously gave his time to teach me numerous plant names and uses, gently putting up with my clumsy pronunciations. Sophie Sherebernikoff and Irene Makarin, both loved and missed, also shared their knowledge with me. I am grateful for the patient work of all these people, past and present, and deeply appreciate all the help I was given. To my husband Benjamin, companion in memory among the wildflowers, and to all my friends and family, this book is your accomplishment as well.

Acknowledgements

Rhododendron camtschaticum Pall., Kamchatka rhododendron

Introduction

The Aleutian Floral Region

Eric Hultén, renowned authority on arctic plants, distinguished four major floral regions in Alaska, yet wrote, "The Aleutian Islands should perhaps be regarded as a fifth floral region" (Hultén 1968). Strewn like seeds in the wind, Alaska's Aleutian Islands are flung out into the stormy North Pacific for eleven hundred miles. The islands break the seas as a spine of volcanic mountains, hemming in the Bering Sea to the north, and reaching in an arc between western North America and eastern Asia. Rugged, windswept, cold and wet, these islands possess a unique vegetation unlike any other on Earth. A thousand miles below the Arctic Circle, the central Aleutians dip farther south than any point in heavily forested southeastern Alaska, yet the islands are a region of treeless tundra.

Throughout the winter months, the islands lie bleak and barren, but in summer a deep green cloaks the hills. Compared with the rest of Alaska, the temperatures are moderate, and the wet maritime climate yields lush plant growth, especially near sea level. While the Aleutians lack mainland Alaska's subzero temperatures and permafrost, they also lack the brief intense warmth of the mainland summers. There is truth to the local quip that we have two seasons here: winter and spring. Mean annual temperature is around 40° F. The only months usually free from a frost at sea level are June, July, and August, and few August days warm above 70° F. By September, the fall gales have begun their long marches across the chain, and the ground cover smolders crimson and ruddy orange beneath the lashing rains. Though temperatures in the coldest winter spells seldom drop below +10° F, the Aleutians are notoriously stormwracked. Low pressure systems sweeping over the Bering Sea bring months of intermittent blizzards and freezing rain. Yet there thrives in the Aleutians a sturdy and diverse world of plants.

So many questions begin to unfold as one studies the life of plants in such a place. Where did they come from? How did they get here? How long have they been here? To consider these things necessitates a brief look back in time, though, in truth, this may reveal more questions than answers. In the Aleutians, much remains a mystery as our knowledge is incomplete; the remaining questions are fascinating and well deserve further study.

The Aleutians are presently treeless, but during the Miocene epoch, five to twenty-five million years ago, temperate forests extended into the islands.

South of Beringia

Geologists date the initial formation of the Aleutians to the late Eocene epoch, around forty million years ago (Drewes et al. 1961). To the north of the island chain lies the now submerged and ancient land bridge known as Beringia. Over the eons, Beringia has recurrently connected Asia and North America as a broad expanse of land. Through vast climatic fluctuations, Beringia has been intermittently inundated and exposed by the rising and falling of the sea. During past exposures plants, animals, and humans have all crossed over it in migrations between the continents (Drewes et al. 1961).

Millions of years ago, however, an entirely different climate and vegetation prevailed. Though one can only imagine what the Aleutian Islands looked like millions or even thousands of years ago, fossil evidence can be revealing. By dating and determining the species that existed in an area, scientists can make inferences about the climate and conditions of the past. During the Miocene epoch, twenty-five to five million years ago, there were trees in the Aleutians. Large petrified trunks have been found on Amchitka Island, and occasionally pieces of petrified wood are found on other islands as well. When these trees were alive, they were part of the temperate forests of conifers and broadleaf deciduous trees that once stretched from Japan up across Beringia and south into Oregon. This is approximately the time when the now-extinct herbivorous sea mammals, Desmostylids, poked around the weedy lagoons of what is now the Unalaska Lake area. Their fossil remains, first discovered in Unalaska valley in the 1950s, have recently been unearthed again in 1994. From what we know, these animals were about the size of ponies and built like hippos. With thick bodies and stout legs, they were probably clumsy on land and foraged in shallow water. Fossils show their forward-pointing tusks protruding from elongated jaws and heavy, cylindrical back teeth (Roland Gangloff, pers. comm.).

While plants, unlike animals, leave few solid remains behind to fossilize, tiny pollen grains and other plant materials that have been preserved as fossils can be used to chart plant history. Core samples of lake sediments, where plant pollen is buried and well preserved, are especially revealing.

The Ice Descends and Retreats

During the Quaternary period (the Pleistocene and our present Holocene epochs), Earth has experienced major climatic fluctuations. The most recent series of glacial ages began around two and a half million years ago, and Earth is now believed to be in a warm interglacial. The last glaciation, often called the Ice Age, reached its peak around 18,000 years ago. While massive glaciers advanced and retreated in North America and northwestern Europe, Beringia itself, which included western and interior Alaska, remained mostly ice free, even at glacial maximums. At the height of both the Illinoian (Riss) glaciation and the more recent Wisconsin glaciation, tremendous ice fields are known to have covered parts of eastern Siberia and most of the Pacific Coast from Oregon northward, including southeastern and southern Alaska and extending westward along the Alaska Peninsula.

As the glaciers advanced, the climate grew colder and drier. The forests of Beringia retreated and the vegetation changed. Whether the land bridge became a region of tundra or grassy arctic steppe is under debate by paleoecologists. We also do not know how similar it may have been to the tundra that exists today. Beringia's ice-free expanse, however, became an enormous refugium, or refuge, for many plant species. Isolated by the barrier of ice to the south and east which covered much of northern North America, Beringia was cut off for a time to migrations from that direction. But it was open to Asia to the west (Hultén 1968).

It was during the glaciations that Beringia lay exposed. During the warmer interglacials, when the ice melted and sea levels rose, the continents would part again. When the glaciers were at their maximum, so much of Earth's water was trapped as glacial ice that sea levels dropped as much as 300 feet. Much of the present continental shelf lay uncovered as a vast Beringian expanse. Even the Pribilof Islands were landlocked for a time, and the Aleutians, from Umnak Island eastward, were united to the Alaska Peninsula, and hence to Beringia and Asia.

It was during these last exposures of the land bridge that people began to cross from Asia into Alaska and North America. The ancestors of the American Indians may have crossed Beringia between 12,000 and 14,000 years ago (R. Knecht, pers. comm.). Recent finds in both North and South America may push these dates back, although sites in Alaska have yet to be linked with earlier migrations. The distinct physical and linguistic differences among Native American groups now suggest that early peoples crossed over from Asia, not all at once, as previously thought, but in numerous migrations over thousands of years (R. Knecht, pers. comm.). Whether they traveled by land or sea and what the conditions were, including the sea levels and the presence of glaciers, remain fascinating questions. What did they hunt and what plants did they gather for food?

The ancestors of the Aleut and Eskimo peoples are believed to have arrived from Asia more recently, perhaps around 10,000 years ago. The two oldest known Aleut village sites lie along what was once the southern coast of Beringia. Recently discovered sites on Hog Island, in Unalaska Bay, have been dated to at least 9,000 years old. Evidence, including charred grass, shows that the site was covered by a pyroclastic flow from nearby Makushin volcano (Dumond and Knecht 2001). The other site, Anangula, equally as old, lies at the western tip of Umnak Island near the present-day village of Nikolski. Anangula then lay near the western tip of the ancient boundaries of the Alaska Peninsula, at the terminus of the land bridge. Situated where the first major oceanic pass then flowed between the Pacific

Hog Island, in Unalaska Bay, once lay along the southern coast of Beringia and the ancient boundaries of the Alaska Peninsula. Archaeologists have dated a village site on the island to at least nine thousand years ago and found evidence the site was blasted by an eruption of nearby Makushin Volcano. The cinder cone of extinct Eider Point Volcano stands in the background.

Makushin Volcano, at 6,680 feet, has an active fumarole and year-round glaciers. The town of Unalaska is about fourteen miles distant.

Ocean and the Bering Sea, funneling marine resources, this area would have provided people with a rich and strategic location (W. S. Laughlin *in* Hopkins 1967).

Whether the entire Aleutian Islands were once covered by glacial ice remains uncertain. While the Illinoian glaciation was more extensive than the more recent Wisconsin, during both episodes the continuous solid ice cover along the southern Alaska coast probably extended no farther west than Unimak Island. Along the Alaska Peninsula, the band of ice cover narrowed. Tongues of glacial ice in the area of Cold Bay have left terminal moraines. But west of Unimak, most islands were probably covered with individual ice caps. Geological surveys done in the Aleutians during the 1950s and 1960s found glacial evidence throughout the islands in landforms such as fjords, and in deposited moraines, arcuate ridges and till. The surveys determined that on Unalaska Island the higher mountains were capped with ice, while smaller glaciers and ice fields lay in the lower parts of the island. The shoreline of Unalaska Island was probably free of shelf ice about 8,000 years ago (Drew et al., 1961; Hamilton & Thorson 1986).

Glaciologists have determined that the snowline in the Aleutians during glacial times was very low. In other words, the elevation to which the snows receded, even in the summer, stayed near sea level, possibly leaving little bare or unfrozen ground. Where glaciers did descend, the existing vegetation perished. There may have been ice-free stretches along the coast in the lee of steep mountains, where descending glaciers parted to reach the sea. Where mountain tops protruded through the ice, in places known as *nunataks*, there would also have been exposed ground. But ice free does not necessarily mean hospitable. Few plants could have survived such harsh conditions as are believed to have existed in the Aleutians during the height of the glaciation (Drew et al., 1961; Hamilton & Thorson 1986).

That the flora in the centrally located islands differs from that found at the eastern and western ends of the Aleutian chain has raised questions among botanists. One speculation, offered by botanist Edward Clebsch of the University of Tennessee, is that if ice fields only extended into the eastern Aleutians, and perhaps, from Asia, into the western islands as well, the central southernmost islands may have remained a refugium, where plants survived until the climate began to warm again. This could explain the number of unique plants found in the central islands (*in* Morgan 1980). Eric Hultén, however, contended: "The flora of the middle Aleutians is very depauperated, probably due to the relatively short time elapsed for plant migration since the glacial period, when most of their plants were exterminated" (Hultén 1960).

Overlooking Constantine Bay and the widespread green of late August.

In September and October, the brilliant colors of fall flame across the hills.

The action of the wind and the resulting pattern of snow accumulation regulates the boundaries of our plant communities.

Plants taking hold on the black volcanic sand of Broad Bay.

A mosaic of plant communities near Morris Cove.

The Migration of Plants

In the Aleutians today there still remains a gap in the circumpolar flora, which is most apparent in the centrally located islands. As Hultén (1960) explains in his *Flora of the Aleutian Islands*, the arctic plants that are widely distributed throughout the world's northern regions are practically absent in the central Aleutians. While many circumpolar and arctic alpine species are present at both ends of the Aleutian chain, the flora of the central islands chiefly consists of Bering Sea and northern Pacific plants. Toward the western end the floristic elements are Asiatic Pacific, and at the eastern end American Pacific. Hultén (1960) was convinced of the links to the west, noting "the islands in phytogeographical respect belong to Asia, as their associations are decidedly Kamtchatkan."

So the pattern of plant life in the Aleutians, as in much of the Northern Hemisphere, has been newly woven since the recent melting of the vast Ice Age glaciers. As the temperatures warmed and the glaciers receded, the land was laid bare. Seeds from both adjacent and distant vegetated regions were blown in, or carried by birds, and slowly plants began to take hold. They did not all arrive at once, or from the same regions. Nor did they become established and spread at the same rate. Plants adapted to different climate conditions and day lengths had to adjust slowly as they pioneered these new areas.

Plants in the Aleutians today are a mingling of immigrants from east and west, survivors from Beringia and *perhaps* from a few scattered refugia throughout the chain. Goldenrod, lupine, kinnikinnick, and yarrow arrived from North America to the east. Iris, purple orchid, Kamchatka rhododendron, and Chukchi primrose came from Asia to the west. Some species like lagotis and Eschscholz buttercup have extended into both ends of the Aleutian chain, but have not yet reached the middle islands. And the rare Aleutian shield fern, *Polystichum aleuticum*, of Adak Island in the central Aleutians, is found nowhere else in the world. The relatively recent migration of plants from Kamchatka into the western Aleutians, and from the Alaska Peninsula into the eastern islands, is exciting for botanists and offers a unique opportunity to study how plants expand their ranges.

The Islands' Diverse Habitats

To observe the diverse plant life in the Aleutian Islands today, which established in such a relatively brief time, confirms the tenacity and adapability of life itself. One ponders how particular species found their scattered and precarious niches, adapted, and continue to persist. The development of our plant communities is also intriguing. Hultén (1960) states,

> It is quite clear that the mosaic of plant communities
> in the Aleutians is to a large extent regulated by the

wind. This wind-plane…is apparently a very important boundary line. However, it is hardly the action of the wind itself that causes the differences. The covering of snow, which is swept away in the places exposed to the wind but accumulates in the unexposed places, is apparently the primary regulating factor. The shelter it gives to the unexposed places enables the more sensitive herbs composing the flora in the meadow to survive, while only the dwarf shrubs and lichens and some few specially hardy herbs can stand the severe conditions in the places that are destitute of snow and exposed to the wind in winter-time.

During chilly Aleutian summers, the diverse habitats of Unalaska yield a profusion of wildflowers. Sea cliffs are speckled with cinquefoil and saxifrage. Along the coast, the beach rye grass is so high one virtually "swims" through it, and monkshood and cow parsnip stand head tall. Back from the beaches, the riverbanks lie under yarrow and violets and the marshes are fringed with orchids, iris, and cotton flowers. Then the foothills rise, split open with wild ravines. Moist meadows, lush with fleabane and cranesbill, lie beneath warming slopes scattered with blueberry bushes. Higher up slope, the meadows retreat to patches in low swales and a dense cover of crowberry heath becomes dominant. Higher yet, the land is broken with rocky outcroppings, ridges, and scree, and scouring winds keep vegetation low. Here, below snowbeds that remain all year, avens, louseworts, and lichens are exposed to the freezing squalls and swirling fog generated by the Bering Sea far below. Within these diverse surroundings are niches for specific wildflowers, each adapted to its unique environment.

Using this Book

The intent of this field guide is to enable identification with a minimal number of botanical terms, while giving the reader interesting details about the plants at hand and a feel for the uniqueness of the Aleutians. Although many of the species included are found throughout the Aleutians, this book is not intended as a comprehensive flora of this vast and remote region.

While some guides arrange the flowers by color or habitat, this one is organized by plant family. Flowers have kin, and by grouping them within families, emphasis is placed on traits that may ease identification. Some, like the iris and violet families, have a sole member on Unalaska, while other families are represented by many species. A few paragraphs on distinguishing characteristics have been included for some of the larger families.

The text for each wildflower is accompanied by a photograph as well as a drawing. The first paragraph describes the plant, giving details to help in identification and comparison with similar species. The second paragraph

Wet meadows and seeps at the base of a slope provide habitat for mosses, ferns, and the more delicate wildflowers, while higher up crowberry and heath take over.

contains information on habitat and range, and whether the plant is edible, poisonous, or known to have medicinal attributes. Other interesting notes and questions that arise are explored. The information on range is provided from the works of Hultén (1960 and 1968); Anderson (1959); Welsh (1974); and Luer (1975). More recent information on range is documented by collections at the University of Alaska Museum Herbarium in Fairbanks. References and the indexes for the botanical, common and Aleut names are offered.

Scientific Names

Common names vary from place to place, while the scientific names give a more reliable and definitive term for any species. Consider crowberries; in Unalaska they are known as mossberries. They're also known locally as blackberries, a translation from the Aleut *qaayum qaxchikluu*. In the mainland U.S., however, blackberry refers to an entirely different plant. Since mossberries are circumpolar, the plant has many names in many languages, but no matter where you are in the world, that plant has only one scientific name: *Empetrum nigrum.*

All plants are grouped into families which in turn are divided into genera (the plural of genus). The first part of a plant's name always begins with a capital letter, and identifies the genus. Along with the second name, which is always in lower case, the individual species within the genus is identified. An example is the salmonberry, a member of the rose family. The scientific name is *Rubus spectabilis*. The nagoonberry, a similar but smaller plant in the same genus, is *Rubus arcticus*. When several species of the same genus are noted in adjacent text, the names may be abbreviated to *R. arcticus* or *R. spectabilis* after the genus *Rubus* is first identified.

Besides being the definitive names for plants, the botanical names often reveal descriptive, mythological, or historical information. A number of local flowers have the species name *unalaschcensis* because they were first collected and described here by naturalists working aboard the ships of early explorers. Sometimes the naturalist's names were given to the plants: *chamissonis, kotzebuei, langsdorffii*. Often the names describe the habitat, appearance, or nature of the flower: *palustris* (of the marsh), *stellaria* (starlike), *procumbens* (trailing on the ground). The word *anemone* is Greek for the wind; *iris* is the word for rainbow.

Over the years, as botanists continue to correct and update the taxonomy of plants, species are occasionally given new scientific names, or have their original names returned to them. The names used by earlier authors are retained and included as synonyms, to assure identification when cross referencing. I have chosen to use as a standard the scientific names given in Eric Hultén's *Flora of Alaska and Neighboring Territories*, first published in 1968. His work remains highly respected and is the one most available to readers. Included in parentheses are any synonyms used in Hultén's earlier work, *Flora of the Aleutian Islands*, 1960; J. P. Anderson's *Flora of Alaska*, 1969; Stanley L. Welsh's *Anderson's Flora of Alaska and Adjacent Parts of Canada*, 1974; as well as the presently accepted names used at the University of Alaska Museum Herbarium in Fairbanks.

The Aleut/Unangan Names and Traditional Uses for Plants

It was the early Russian explorers who first began to use the term Aleut for the Native people living in the Aleutian Islands. Although the name has been used for a long time, recently the Aleut people have begun to replace it with a term from their own language, and to call themselves Unangan or Unangas, depending on the dialect. Just as the words Yup'ik and Iñupiaq are more frequently and correctly being used in place of the word Eskimo, this change comes from an ongoing recognition of the need to preserve a sense of cultural pride and identity.

The Unangan language is soft-spoken and wonderfully descriptive. It was once spoken throughout the Aleutian Islands and along the Alaska Peninsula about as far east as Port Moller and the Shumagin Islands. As many as nine distinct dialects once existed within the island groups. Two of these dialects, often termed Eastern and Atkan, are still being spoken today, although for the most part only the elders are still fluent in their language. Linguistically, the Unangan language is related to Eskimo, a language family totally separate from Athabaskan/Eyak/Tlingit. As with many of Alaska's and indeed the world's indigenous languages, the use of Unangan has greatly declined within the last few generations. Current interest in preserving the language is encouraging, however, and it is now being taught in some of the region's schools.

Due to the various dialects, plant names differ between Aleutian villages. Unangan readers are sure to know names and spellings other than those given, and any errors are mine. Wherever possible, the dialectic origins of the names are included: (E) for Eastern and (A) for Atkan. In both dialects the singular ending for a noun is x̂. Interestingly, the language also includes a dual ending, in which a pair of things (people, ducks, mittens) is recognized by the ending *x* without the circumflex (ˆ). Under the influence of English, this ending is not used much anymore. The plural ending in the Eastern dialect is *n*, and in the Atkan dialect, *s*. An example is *ulax̂*, which means house or dwelling. *Ulan*, with the Eastern plural ending, means dwellings. When combined with another word and used in a possessive form, the endings of both words change. An example is *aanasnaadam ulaa*, the bumblebee's house, the descriptive name for the monkshood flower. *Aanasnaadax̂*, bumblebee, is given the relative or possessive ending *m* and *ulax̂* becomes *ulaa*. A pronunciation guide is provided in the back of the book.

The Unangan names for plants can be fascinating and often amusing. The clever likenesses people saw in the plants are especially intriguing—the wild iris petals as whale flukes, the lupine's long root as the land's spike, the cottonflower... the goose's what? Because the names have been carried down from antiquity, they sometimes refer to things long gone now, providing an insight into the past. The watermelon berry, for example, which has edible but very watery fruit, was given the name water container, or water bag: *taangadgusix̂*. In the days before plastic, this would have been a seal or sea lion stomach, carried in the *iqyax̂*, or kayak.

The descriptive terms for the plants reveal an intimate connection, awareness, and knowledge attained over many generations. Not only the names have been carried from the past, but also the acquired wisdom about plants' uses for food and medicine. The medicinal attributes of plants had to be learned by trial and error, practiced and passed on over countless generations. The Unangan people had remedies for healing wounds and infections, medicines for the eyes and skin, for digestion and internal disorders. Although many of our local plants still retain their medicinal reputations, most of the information about their preparation and administration has been lost and forgotten. For this reason a strong word of caution is due: be very careful using plants you are unfamiliar with; some are harmful, or can be if not used properly.

Rooted in Aleutian Soil

Whether you are gathering wild plants for food, medicine, or simply learning their names, that knowledge connects you at once to the land. Some of this knowledge could prove indispensable if you get caught out hiking somewhere in this rugged country. Highly nutritious greens, roots, and berries await you. Yarrow will help stop bleeding if you get hurt. Dry grass will keep your feet warm if your socks get soaked, and you can avoid water underfoot altogether by recognizing vegetation typical of wet ground.

The Aleutians are a rugged place; the land is rough and the weather dependably grueling. It is also a fragile environment, though some people have treated it harshly. The tundra still retains the scars of World War II, for recovery is slow in these cold soils. As roads crisscross what once were blooming meadows and marshes, vegetation no longer serves to filter now-muddied lakes and streams. Beach banks and dunes are held together with the tangled roots of salt-tolerant species, like wild rye and beach pea. Once the plants are destroyed, the land soon succumbs to pulling seas and winds; the ensuing erosion is costly, and often impossible, to repair. Decades will pass before the ground cover of heather and kinnikinnick heals the holes in the hills from gravel quarrying.

The Aleutian wilderness remains unique on an Earth fast losing its wild places. Yet, remote as these islands appear to be, we have learned that all places on Earth are connected, be it the rain forests, Antarctica, or the

Bering Sea. In protecting the resources that sustain us, knowledge of our surroundings is our strongest tool. In the midst of uncertain times there is welcome reassurance in the return of wildflowers each spring, and the opportunity to learn more about them. My hope is this book will guide you on your own journeys.

Benjamin Golodoff with taangadgusin, *or watermelon berry,* Streptopus amplexifolius.

Plant Descriptions

Sedge Family / *Cyperaceae*

The sedges, along with the closely related grasses (*Gramineae*), and rushes (*Juncaceae*), are fascinating and beautiful plants, with many members in the Aleutians. Although they are all flowering plants, only two sedges (cotton flowers) are included in this book. The remainder are often more difficult to identify.

**Cotton Flower,
Cotton Grass**
*Eriophorum
angustifolium* Honck.

Emerging from underground rhizomes, the single stems are thin, stiff, usually 4" to 18" tall. The leaves are long and linear, folded lengthwise near the tips. The cottony spikes are numerous and often nodding, with soft white bristles.

Blooming across marshes and wet meadows, *E. angustifolium* is one of two common cotton flowers in our area. It is easily distinguished from *E. russeolum* by its multiple silky white tassels and shorter, more delicate, slender green stems. The lower part of the stem is edible and sweet tasting when gathered in the spring.

RANGE:
Northern circumpolar and widespread in Alaska.

Cotton Flower, Cotton Grass, Russett Cotton Grass
Eriophorum russeolum Fries.
(E, A) *lagim ichx̂uusii*: goose's toilet paper
(E) *tumĝasix̂*

19

Emerging from underground rhizomes, the stems are long, stiff and slender, 12" to 28" tall. The leaves are long and linear. The stems bear a single upright, cottony spike of soft, rust-colored bristles.

This cotton flower's single round, ivory puff has a rusty tinge, hence the humorous Aleut name. Blooming in marshes and wetlands, often among iris (*Iris setosa*) and bog orchids (*Platanthera* spp.), it sometimes covers vast patches, like summer snow fields. If picked before the seed loosens, cotton flowers can be hung upside down until the stems dry straight, and made into winter bouquets.

RANGE:
Northern circumpolar and widespread in Alaska.

Sedge Family / *Cyperaceae*

Lily Family / *Liliaceae*

Lilies emerge from rhizomes, bulbs, or corms. The leaves are oblong to linear in shape with parallel veins. The flower parts are in threes or multiples of three. Often the petals and sepals look alike and are known as "tepals." The flowers are often showy, developing fruit as a capsule or berry.

Northern Asphodel
Tofieldia coccinea Richards

Arising from a rootstock of numerous pale, wiry roots, the flowering stems are smooth and upright, usually less than 4" tall. The stems bear one or more narrow leaves, at least one of them being fairly well developed. The basal leaves, arranged in a fan-shaped tuft, are stiff, narrow and pointed, usually less than 2" long. The tiny flowers are held in a single, short dense cluster at the top of the stem. The flowers are whitish, tinged with reddish purple. The fruit is a small, dry capsule.

The northern asphodel bears such small and short-stemmed flowers that it is often the stiff, fan-shaped tuft of leaves that catches your eye. It usually grows in dry tundra where the vegetation is low, among the lichens and pussy toes (*Antennaria* spp.) of rocky outcroppings, but occasionally can be found in damp heath as well.

A similar but less commonly seen species here is the Scotch or false asphodel, *Tofieldia pusilla* (Michx.) Pers. Its flowers are yellowish white to greenish, and it usually bears a smaller, much less well-developed stem leaf than does *T. coccinea.*

RANGE:
Both species are northern circumpolar and widespread in Alaska.

21

Scotch Asphodel, Tofieldia pusilla

Kamchatka Lily, Rice Root, Chocolate Lily, Stinky Flower, Sarana Lily
Fritillaria camschatcensis (L.) Ker Gawl.

(E) *saranax̂*, from the Russian sarana
(E, A) *alugax̂*: the root bulb, *alugam kangaa*: the above-ground part
(A) *daax̂sxingis*: the rice-like grains around the root

Stems are single, smooth, 12" to 28" tall. Leaves are lanceolate, blunt, held in widely spaced whorls along the stem. Bunched at the top are one to several large, nodding, bell-shaped flowers with a rather unpleasant scent. The petals are dark purple brown, sometimes streaked with green. After flowering, the plants form smooth, inch-long capsules, which are obtusely angled into three sections. Below the ground at the base of the stem is a round, white root bulb covered with small bulblets, resembling a cluster of rice.

Kamchatka lilies bloom in the meadows and hillsides in early to mid summer. The edible root bulbs are best gathered in early fall and are good boiled, tasting much like potatoes. The sometimes bitter taste of the roots can be lessened by soaking them in fresh water. The traditional method of dipping or storing them in seal oil is also said to sweeten them (M. Dirks, pers. com.). These roots were widely used as food in the past. They were boiled, roasted, or fried and were good mixed with berries. They could also be dried and later ground into a flour (Hudson 1992).

RANGE:
Widespread from eastern Asia, along the southern Alaska coast and into the Pacific Northwest.

The root bulbs of Kamchatka, or rice root lily, gathered in the fall. Note that the flowers are gone and seed capsules have formed at this stage.

Alp Lily
Llyodia serotina (L.) Rchb.

The small bulb and base of stem are sheathed in grass-like fibers. The flowering stems are 2" to 6" tall. The basal leaves are linear, long, and curving, and often longer than the flowering stem. Stem leaves are alternate, becoming smaller up the stem. The flower is usually solitary and ½" in diameter. The six rounded tepals are creamy white, faintly tinged with yellow, and have purplish brown streaks or veins, the midvein being especially prominent. The fruit is a small three-sided capsule.

The alp lily is a delicate little bloom of the alpine tundra, uncommon on Unalaska Island. It is found sparsely scattered among the heath-covered rocky outcroppings at higher elevations.

RANGE:
Northern circumpolar and widespread in Alaska.

**Watermelon Berry, Wild
Cucumber, Twisted Stalk**
Streptopus amplexifolius
(L.) DC.

(E) *taangadgusin* (from
taangax̂: water): the berries of the plant; also the
term for water container or
water bag, originally a seal
or sea lion stomach. *Taan-
gadgusim ulingin*: leaves of
the plant
(A) *taanamchiizax̂,
taangamchiidax̂*

Arising from a stout rhizome, the branching stems
are long, bending and twisting, 12" to 40" tall. The
lower part of the stem is covered with firm, stiff hairs.
The leaves are large and glabrous, ovate to broadly lanceolate. They are held alternately along the stems, clasping and
nearly encircling them. Beneath most leaves is one tiny bell-like,
white to pinkish-yellow flower hanging on a short thread-like stem. In
late summer, they ripen into elongated, smooth-skinned, bright red fruits,
which hang in a row on the stems. Watermelon berry is found widely scattered among ferns and other tall growth, usually in damp meadows and
beneath slopes; it seems
particular about its hab-
itat. The young tender
shoots have a cucum-
ber-like taste. The berries
are also edible and sweet
but very watery, as the
Unangan name implies.

RANGE:
Northern circumpolar
and widespread in Alaska
south of the Arctic Circle.

Fruits of the watermelon berry

Iris Family / *Iridaceae*

Wild Iris, Wild Flag
Iris setosa Pall.

(E) *nuusnuchx̂aadan*: scissors flower, a name also given to the monkshood (A) *umsutuudax̂*, from the root word *umsux̂:* fluke, whale's tail, whale flipper, and in other forms, the word for tongue, and the blade of a paddle (most likely in reference to the shape of the petals).

Growing from a woody rootstock, the stems are smooth, thick, 12" to 16" tall. The stems branch once or twice near the top. The leaves are long, flat and narrowly lance shaped. The deep purple flowers unfurl three velvety petals, each feathered with white at the center. The petals are spreading, broadly rounded, narrowing at the flower's center. The unopened flowers are curled into long dark purple tips encased in green sheaths. Later, large three-sided seed pods form at the top of the plant.

During the grip of winter, when these islands lie bleak and frozen, it is hard to imagine such an exotic-looking flower existing in the Aleutians. In midsummer, the irises bloom in wet meadows, on damp hillsides and along the edges of lakes and marshes. They often grow among fleabane *(Erigeron peregrinus)*, cotton flowers *(Eriophorum* spp.) and ferns. The plant is poisonous and will cause vomiting, although the Unangan learned to use it medicinally. The roots were boiled for a tea used to treat gastric disorders and as a strong laxative (Bank 1962).

RANGE:
Eastern Asia and coastal Alaska.

Orchid Family / *Orchidaceae*

Orchids emerge from bulbs, corms, rhizomes, or tuberous roots. Nearly all Aleutian orchids have very fragrant roots, even those with blossoms that have no fragrance. Many have a symbiotic relationship between their roots and certain fungi. For this reason, and the fact that many are rare species, it is best not to try transplanting them. The leaves of orchids are usually simple and entire, and they often sheathe the stem. The flowers are composed of three sepals and three petals, a deceptively simple theme which the family has evolved into a diversity of exquisite flowers. The three sepals are usually alike and are often colored, resembling the petals or the bracts. Of the three petals, two are alike and held laterally like wings. The third and lower petal is usually markedly different, giving the flower its irregular shape. This lower petal forms a pouch in some species, as in the lady slipper *(Cypripedium guttatum)*, or a lip which is often flared and sometimes includes a spur. Orchids are insect pollinated, and this showy lip is an inviting place to alight. In the Aleutians, the small orchids are often pollinated by mosquitoes. (A handy thing to remember when you wonder why on Earth we need mosquitos.) The orchid's fruit is a capsule containing a large number of tiny seeds.

About a dozen species of orchids are found in the Aleutian Islands, and some are quite rare. A few are showy and highly fragrant; the most common and well known locally are the lady's slipper, the purple orchid *(Dactylorhiza aristata)* and the bog orchids *(Platanthera* spp.*)*. A number of smaller yet equally exquisite species grow in scattered locations in the damp meadows and slopes, often hidden within the heath.

The origins and migrations of Aleutian orchids are fascinating to trace. The Aleutians have provided the stepping stones between Asia and North America for many northern species. Our purple orchid is a rarity in much of Alaska; it is suspected to have migrated from Asia across the Aleutian Chain, reaching only just beyond the Alaska Peninsula to Kodiak Island and Prince William Sound. Another probable migrant from the west is the Bering bog orchid *(Platanthera tipuloides)*. Regarded as one of North America's rarest orchids, it is found only in Japan, Kamchatka, and the Aleutians. While reportedly quite common on the westernmost Aleutian island of Attu (Luer 1975), it has only recently been found as far east as Unalaska Island, where it is very rare.

For other orchids, we are the westernmost outpost of migrations from
North America. Alaska piperia *(Platanthera unalaschcensis)* occurs along
the Pacific Coast but is not known west of Unalaska. Hooded ladies' tresses
(Spiranthes romanzoffiana), widespread across Canada and the western
United States, occurs no further west than the central Aleutians. Our
white bog orchid *(Platanthera dilatata)*, also widespread in North America, can be found throughout the chain and also in Kamchatka and Japan.
The Aleutian Islands are remote and relatively little explored, and range
extensions continue to be recorded.

Orchids are comparatively scarce in cool climates, with perhaps 140
species in North America and less than thirty in Alaska. However, there
are well over 20,000 individual species of orchids worldwide, distributed
mainly in the tropics, making them the largest family of flowering plants.

*Low-lying wetlands in the Aleutians provide excellent orchid habitat and are
particularly favored by the bog orchids or* Platantheras.

Orchid Family / *Orchidaceae*

Lady's Slipper
Cypripedium guttatum Sw.

The rootstock is long and horizontal with emerging tubers. Two large, broadly elliptic leaves clasp the single flowering stem. The stem is slender and upright, 6" to 8" tall, and covered with short glandular hairs. A small leafy bract appears behind the flower. The single, delicate flower can be described as having a pouch below, a hood above and two ears. The flower is usually creamy white and mottled with purplish brown. Color variation occurs within the species, ranging from white to pinkish blotched with greenish purple or purple.

Lady's slipper often blooms on hillsides, among wintergreen *(Pyrola* spp.), bistort *(Polygonum viviparum),* and fleabane *(Erigeron peregrinus).* Locals love to go searching for them early each summer. Unfortunately, the ground squirrels can't wait for them either, so often you will spot the familiar leaves, the slender stem, but no flower.

RANGE:
Eurasia, the Aleutians, interior Alaska, and the Yukon.

Purple Orchid, Showy Orchid

Dactylorhiza aristata
(Fisch.) Soo
(= *Orchis aristata* Fisch.)

(E) *quungdiix̂*: This is also the word for monkshood (both plants are known to be toxic); *tungsungax̂*

Emerging from thick, forked tubers, the flowering stems are smooth and 5" to 8" tall. The leaves are lance shaped, up to 4" long, and often have dark purplish brown spots. The flowers are showy, held in a short spike and are rose purple, occasionally pink, or very rarely white.

Purple orchids bloom very early in the spring, first appearing on south-facing hillsides and meadows. The earliest of them seem to flower on very short stems, because, unlike many other plants whose leaves appear first, the purple orchid's flowers push right out of the ground. Unlike the taller bog orchids, the flowers are not fragrant, and the plant is thought to be poisonous.

RANGE:
Eastern Asia, the Aleutians, Alaska Peninsula to Prince William Sound.

Bog Orchid, Cornflower
*Platanthera convallariae-
folia (Fischer) Lindley*

chaxitxam kangaa, from
chaxilix: to dig out; and
kangaa: above

Emerging from a thick, elongated, tuber-like root, the single stems are smooth and hollow, 4" to 20" tall. The leaves are long and lance shaped, clasping the lower stem, becoming smaller and narrower up the stem until they resemble the narrow bracts crowded within the flowering spike. The long spike of pale greenish-yellow flowers is very fragrant. While many plants grow to only a foot high, some get as tall as three feet and quite stout. They do look like small corn stalks, hence the common name.

Bog orchids bloom in the marshy meadows in early to mid summer. Distinguished from the white bog orchid *(P. dilatata)* by its greenish rather than snow-white flowers, the cornflower is also often more robust and blooms earlier. The two species are quite distinct on Unalaska Island, but there has been considerable discussion regarding names and hybridization of these orchids. The Unangan used the edible roots of both these orchids for food. They were said to be best steamed, and could be cooked covered with putchki *(Heracleum lanatum)* leaves.

RANGE:
Kamchatka, the Aleutians, to Prince William Sound.

White Bog Orchid, Bog Candles

Platanthera dilatata
(Pursh) Lindl.
(=*Habenaria dilatata*
(Pursh) Hook.,
Limnorchis dilatata
(Pursh) Rydb.)

(E) *chaxitxax̂, tugdukax̂*
(A) *chagitxax̂*

Emerging from a thick, elongated, tuber-like root, the single stems are smooth and hollow, usually less than 14" tall. The leaves are long and lance shaped, clasping the lower stem, becoming smaller and narrower up the stem until they resemble the narrow bracts crowded within the flowering spike. The long spike of snow-white flowers is highly perfumed.

White bog orchids grace the marshy meadows and wetlands. They are very similar to the greenish bog orchid (*P. convallariaefolia*), but the flowers are snow white, and the plant is usually smaller and more delicate. It is also later blooming, and the fragrance is distinct, more perfumed than the greenish bog orchid. The Unangan gathered and steamed the roots of both these orchids for food.

RANGE:
North America, Pacific coast of Alaska and throughout the Aleutians.

Bering Bog Orchid
Platanthera tipuloides (L.)
Lindl.
var. *behringiana* (Ryd-
berg) Hult.
(=*Habenaria behringiana*
(Rydb.) Ames., *Limnor-
chis behringiana* Rydb.)

Emerging from a forked
and fleshy tuber-like root,
the single stem is up to
7½" tall. The stem is
smooth and upright,
rounded below the leaves,
squared and striate above
them. The one or two
leaves are elliptic to lance
shaped, up to 4" long and
¾" wide, shiny on the up-
per surface and with a duller sheen beneath. The lower leaf sheathes
the stem and is larger than the upper leaf. The flowering spike is up
to 2" long, only faintly fragrant, and bearing up to twenty flowers.
The leaf-like bracts are long and narrow; the lower ones the
longest at almost an inch, and twice as long as the flowers. The
flower's petals are golden yellow, (not purplish as described
by some of the early authors). The sepals are yellowish green.
The spur is fully ½" long, thin and curving.

The Bering bog orchid is regarded as one of
North America's rarest orchids. While reportedly quite common on Attu Island (Luer 1975), it has only
recently been recorded as far east as Unalaska Island (ALA Collection; C. Parker, pers. comm.), where it is known from only one site. It
was found blooming in late July in a wet and mossy meadow in Unalaska
valley.

As with the other species of *Platanthera*, the flower parts are very
small, but the Bering bog orchid's long, thin and curving spur is easily
noted. The yellow flowers, their lack of strong fragrance, and the plant's
small size also distinguish it from the other bog orchids.

RANGE:
Japan, Kamchatka, and the Aleutians.

Choris Bog Orchid
Platanthera chorisiana
(Cham.) Rchb.
(= *Habenaria chorisiana*
Cham., *Limnorchis
chorisiana* (Cham.) J. P.
Anders.)

Emerging from a fleshy thickened root, the glabrous, grooved stem is 2½" to 6" tall, and often slightly bending.

The two oval leaves near the base of the stem have a shiny upper surface, and the lower leaf is rounder and wider where it meets the stem, relative to the upper leaf. A small, narrow leaf-like bract appears on the upper stem. The flowers are fragrant, greenish, and very small, the sepals and petals short and blunt and the petals nearly closed into a tiny sphere.

Although reportedly quite common on Attu Island (Luer 1975), the tiny Choris orchid is on the Alaska rare plant list (Alaska Natural Heritage Program 2001). On Unalaska Island, it is not so much a rarity as simply difficult to find. This very small green-colored orchid blooms in late July, but is often nearly hidden in the damp mossy tundra and heath (*Ericaceae*). The plant was named for Louis Choris, the Russian artist who traveled in the Aleutians in the early 1800s.

RANGE:
Japan, the Aleutians, along the Alaska coast, and southward to Washington.

Alaska Piperia, Alaska Bog Orchid

Platanthera unalaschcensis (Spreng.) Kurtz
(= *Piperia unalaschcensis* (Spreng.) Rydb., *Habenaria unalashcensis* (Spreng.) Wats.)

Alaska piperia is easily distinguished from the other small orchids by its sweetish but disagreeable smell. Emerging from a tuber-like root, the single stem is slender, glabrous, grooved, and 6" to 10" tall. The two to three basal leaves are oblong to lanceolate, and 1 ½" to 2 ½" long. The upper stem bears two to three small and narrow leaf-like bracts. The bract below each flower is much shorter than the flower itself. The flowers are pale greenish and numerous, often more than twenty, and held in a tall narrow spike. Both the petals and sepals are greenish, and the spur is short and slender, about as long as the flower's lower lip.

Alaska piperia is uncommon here and seems to prefer dry tundra, often near the beach. At first the scent seems sweet, but it soon hits you with an ammonia-like pungency. The first collection of this orchid was made in Unalaska by Chamisso, the poet-naturalist and botanist sailing with Kotzebue in 1816–1817 aboard the ship *Rurik*.

⌐ RANGE:
In scattered populations from Unalaska Island eastward, along the southern Alaska coast into North America.

Hooded Ladies' Tresses
Spiranthes romanzoffiana
Cham.

Emerging from a fleshy, thickened root, the single stem is stout and usually less than 6" tall. The lower leaves are long and lance-olate. Smaller leafy bracts appear on the stem and are densely crowded between the flowers. The creamy white flowers are held in a spike composed of three spiraling rows. In this orchid, the sepals and petals form a hooded tube and the flower lacks a spur.

This small, spicy-scented flower looks something like a short bog orchid, with its lance-shaped leaves and spike of blooms. The flowers, however, form an unusual twisted spiral. It is often so short that its flowers seem to twist right out of the ground. Not as common as the bog orchids, it prefers drier areas where the vegetation is low, such as roadsides and tundra.

RANGE:
Widespread across Canada, the western United States and Alaska, as far as the central Aleutians.

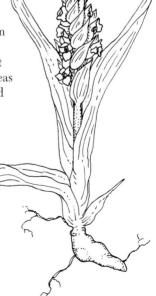

Orchid Family / Orchidaceae

Broad-leaved Twayblade,
Swan Orchid
Listera convallarioides
(Sw.) Nutt.

Emerging from fleshy, fibrous roots, the flowering stem is single and up to 6" tall. The two leaves, held near the middle of the stem, are glabrous and broadly oval, and 1" to 2 ½" long. Below the leaves the stem is thicker and glabrous; above the leaves the stem is sparsely pubescent. The flowers are pale greenish yellow, widely spaced, and held on short, bracted pedicels. The flower's lip is wedge-shaped and up to ½" long.

This exquisite and seldom-seen orchid blooms in July on Unalaska Island, in the heath-covered foothills, often among twinflowers (*Linnaea borealis*), bistort (*Polygonum viviparum*), and fleabane (*Erigeron peregrinus*). The flower looks remarkably like a tiny swan, with a long curving neck, uplifted wings, and the long lip extending from the swan's breast.

RANGE:
Scattered in disjunct populations across the United States and Canada. In Alaska, known from the Aleutian Islands, Alaska Peninsula, and southeast Alaska (ALA collections; C. Parker pers. comm.).

Pale green and rose-purple heart-leaved twayblade

Heart-leaved Twayblade
  Listera cordata (L.) R. Br.
  (= *Ophrys cordata* L.)

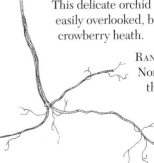

Emerging from fleshy, fibrous roots, the single stem is very slender, 4" to 8" tall. A single pair of heart-shaped leaves is held at mid stem. The leaves are up to 1 ½" long and wide. The stem is slightly thicker below the leaves, and slightly pubescent just above them. Sparsely flowered, the tiny blooms have three narrow sepals and two similar petals, the third lower petal forming a long forked lip or beard. Some plants have pale greenish flowers and stems, while others are a dark rose purple, and the two often grow together.

   Heart-leaved twayblade blooms early to mid-season and often grows on damp hillsides. This delicate orchid is fairly common, though easily overlooked, being nearly hidden in the crowberry heath.

   RANGE:
      Northern circumpolar in distribution, found throughout the Aleutians.

Early or Northern Coral-root
Corallorhiza trifida Chat.

This plant emerges from a pale, coral-like rhizome. The stems are glabrous, pale greenish to purplish, and 2" to 10" tall. Lacking leaves, the stems are sheathed with two or more bracts. The flowers, held in a loose cluster, are few, weakly scented, and small. The petals and sepals are narrow, greenish yellow to purplish brown, and about ¼" long. The lip is shorter and rounded, white and often with tiny reddish purple spots. The capsule is oval shaped, narrowing at both ends and about ⅜" long.

This small fascinating orchid is uncommon in Unalaska and is easily overlooked because of its inconspicuous color. The coral-roots are saprophytic plants, deriving nutrients from decaying organic matter. Because of this they lack chlorophyll and hence the dark green color of most other plants that make their own food. The rootstock is a pale, brittle coral-like mass, actually an underground stem which sprouts new plants. It favors damp muddy or rocky soil, wetlands and meadows, and blooms in early to midsummer.

RANGE:
Northern circumpolar and widespread in Alaska; eastern Aleutians only.

White Adder's Tongue, Adder's Mouth
Malaxis monophylla (L.) Sw.
(= *Microstylis monophyllos* (L.) Lindl.)

Emerging from a hard, round, greenish, bulb-like corm, the stems are a pale yellowish green, glabrous, squared, and narrowly grooved. They stand 4" to 9" tall. At the lower part of the stem are one or two long-sheathed leaves. The one main leaf is broadly elliptic to lanceolate, and 1" to 3" long. The second leaf varies in size; it may be nearly as large as the main leaf, or just a suggestion of a leaf. The flowers are pale yellowish green, numerous but very tiny, and held in a terminal spike.

An uncommon orchid here, white adder's tongue grows in small scattered patches and often in gravelly soil. The flowers bloom in mid to late July.

RANGE:
Northern circumpolar in distribution, although not recorded in the central Aleutian Islands, where there seems to be a gap in its range.

Willow Family / *Salicaceae*

Willows are known by their slender twigs, short-stalked leaves and often pubescent (short fuzzy) or villose (long fuzzy) showy "pussy willow" catkins. During the winter each bud on the twig is protected under a single scale. Depending on the species, the catkins come out before or with the leaves. Although they have no petals and only bloom for a short time in the spring, the catkins are actually clusters of very small flowers. All the

individual flowers in a willow catkin are either male or female. Likewise, all the catkins on one shrub are the same sex, so shrubs themselves are either male or female. When they first come out, both male and female catkins tend to be fuzzy. The male flowers develop pollen-bearing stamens. The female flowers receive the pollen through their tiny, extended stigmas, and later develop pointed seed capsules. These capsules split open to release tiny, down-tufted seeds (see photo, left). Both male and female flowers produce nectar that attracts pollinating insects.

The young leaves, shoots, and inner bark of some species are sweet-tasting and high in vitamin C. In northern Alaska, the Native people traditionally stored young petruski (*Ligusticum scoticum*) and diamondleaf willow (*Salix pulchra*) leaves in seal oil, and the method kept both the oil and the leaves fresh (Jones 1981). The bark of many willows is bitter-tasting, due to the salicin, or natural aspirin, it contains. Long known for its pain-relieving and anti-inflammatory abilities, our modern aspirin is a chemically derived synthetic of the substance originally found in willows. Although aspirin is faster acting, herbalists find willow bark teas, tinctures, and salves to be effective and lacking the side effects of the synthetic drug.

At least thirty-three species of willows have been identified in Alaska, and they are adapted to a wide range of conditions. They occur throughout the state, including the Aleutian Islands, where half a dozen species have been recorded. For purposes of identification, they are often separated into dwarf and shrub categories. Low-growing or dwarf willows are gnarled, prostrate woody plants often found clinging to windy ridges and knolls. The taller shrub willows often grow in dense thickets, fringing

streams and lakes in the valleys. In protected areas some species of shrub willows can become small trees.

Though willows are easily distinguished from other plants, the identification to species is notoriously difficult. To begin with, many morphological characteristics of willows are highly variable. Also, many species hybridize, and this may even occur between the dwarf and shrub willows. Some of the shrub species that are tall where sheltered may be dwarfed if growing in an exposed habitat. Thus, height alone is not always a reliable characteristic.

Identification generally requires close examination of both the mature leaves and the catkins, but they often do not appear on the twig at the same time. One technique is to observe the catkins when they appear, mark the bush with a ribbon, and later in the season return to observe the mature leaves. The young leaves of many willows are pubescent, only later developing their distinguishing mature characteristics, smooth upper surfaces or whitish undersides.

Identification of willows is difficult, even for the experts. Their variability can amaze as well as frustrate, and many people are happy to know it is a willow and leave it at that. The best approach is with a good key. Recommended are *Alaska Trees and Shrubs* by Viereck and Little (1972), and the *Salix* key contributed by George Argus found in Welsh's *Flora of Alaska and Adjacent Parts of Canada* (1974). On the following pages, descriptions and separate keys have been provided for the willows found in the Aleutians.

Dwarf Willows

Salix species

(E) *tanam kayuu, tanam kayungin:* creeping willow, from *tanax:* ground and *kayux̂:* any muscle, strength or power, a rootlet
(E) *usx̂ix̂:* willow
(E) *usx̂im kayungin*

The low-growing dwarf willows are seldom more than a few inches high. Their crawling branches hug the ground like nature's bonsais, often forming dense mats, twisting and trailing their branches through mossy and stony tundra, or clinging to bare, rocky outcroppings at high elevations. In these windy, exposed locations the worn and gnarled branches are incredibly strong and sometimes as thick as a wrist. One wonders how old some of them are. Alaska botanist Carolyn Parker tells me that some arctic willows *(Salix arctica)* from Greenland are approximately 130 years old.

Two of the dwarf willows, the netleaf willow *(Salix reticulata)* and the arctic willow *(Salix arctica),* are common and fairly easy to identify. The other two species found in the Aleutians are the oval leaf willow *(Salix ovalifolia)* and the least willow *(Salix rotundifolia).*

The following key will help separate them. The key is not foolproof, however, and once a species has been determined using the key, other morphological characters should be checked to confirm its identification. Be alert for shrub willows displaying a dwarf growth form in exposed habitats and for hybrids between dwarf and shrub species.

Key to dwarf willows found on Unalaska Island:

Choose between A1 and A2.

A1. Leaves conspicuously net veined and rough textured, slender catkins borne on normal leafy shoots: See netleaf willow, *Salix reticulata*.

A2. Leaves not conspicuously net veined, smooth textured, catkins borne on short leafy shoots. Choose between B1 and B2.

B1. Branches often ascending 4" to 12" tall. Leaves usually more than 1" long. Catkins usually more than 1 ½" long, thick and many-flowered, ovaries hairy: See arctic willow, *Salix arctica*.

B2. Branches usually less than 4" tall. Leaves less than 1" long. Catkins less than 1 ½" long, ovaries glabrous. Choose between C1 and C2.

C1. Upper surface of leaves shiny green, under surface pale to whitish. Catkins many-flowered, ¾" to 1 ½" long. Forming colonies by layering. Leaves not persistent more than one year. See oval leaf willow, *Salix ovalifolia* (=*S. stolonifera*).

C2. Leaves shiny green on both surfaces, not whitish beneath. Catkins few-flowered, ½" long. Forming colonies by underground stems. Leaves often persistent more than one year. See least willow, *Salix rotundifolia*.

Netleaf Willow, Netted Willow, Net-Veined Willow
Salix reticulata L.

LEAVES: Up to 1 ½" long, nearly round to oval in shape. Leaves are leathery and rough-textured with a network of veins which are raised on the under surface. The upper surface is dark glossy green.

CATKINS: Up to 2" long, slender and reddish purple, and borne on long leafless stalks.

Netleaf willow grows among the mosses and crowberry heath plants, often at upper elevations. The branches do not form dense mats, and often just the leaves show above the surrounding vegetation.
The net-veined leaves distinguish it from other willows, but they could easily be mistaken for alpine bearberry *(Arctostaphylos alpina)* leaves, and the two plants favor the same habitat. On the netleaf willow the base of the leaf is distinctly rounded where it meets the stem, whereas the bearberry's leaf tapers to its stem.

Oval leaf willow, male catkins

Oval leaf willow, female catkins

Oval Leaf Willow
Salix ovalifolia Trautv.
(including *S. stolonifera* Cov.)

LEAVES: ⅜" to 1" long, elliptic to round, the leaf base variable. Upper surface glossy green, under surface pale green to whitish. Leaves may be sparsely pubescent, but no long hairs extend beyond the leaf tip, as they often do in the arctic willow *(S. arctica)*.

CATKINS: many-flowered, ¾" to 1½" long, on leafy shoots.

This willow sends out long slender stems, either trailing on the surface or underground. These stems produce yellowish roots where they touch the ground. Oval leaf willow grows along open beaches and the shores of marshes. Some authors separate *S. ovalifolia* from *S. stolonifera* but with admitted difficulty. Others suggest the two are variants of one species. The scientific name *stolonifera* means 'with stolons,' which are horizontal stems or runners.

Least Willow
Salix rotundifolia Trautv.

LEAVES: Less than ½" long, round, ovate to elliptic, both surfaces smooth and glossy, the primary veins prominently raised.

Catkins: Few-flowered (4–15) and ½" long.

This is a densely matted ground willow whose stems radiate from a central taproot. Branch tips often erect. Least willow often prefers alpine tundra but it may also be found in small, open sites within moist meadows and crowberry heath at all elevations. The tiny, compact and low-growing plants can be easily overlooked.

Male catkin

Arctic Willow, Ground Willow
Salix arctica Pall.

LEAVES: Size and shape extremely diverse, ¾" to nearly 3" long. Leaves generally rounded, varying from obovate to elliptic. Upper surface dark green and shiny, under surface pale green. Margins entire (not toothed). Young leaves often villose, later becoming glabrous (hairless); mature leaves often bearded, with long hairs extending beyond the leaf tip.

Female catkin

CATKINS: Tall and erect, 1" to 4" long, much longer than the other dwarf willow catkins. Note the tiny red stigmas that look like bird's feet on the female catkin in the photograph.

The Arctic willow is extremely variable in form and thrives in a diversity of habitats, from moist meadows to rocky alpine tundra. The low-growing gnarled branches crawl over the ground and often form dense mats, but in protected places the branches may stand 12" high or more. It is suspected to hybridize not only with other dwarf willows but also with some shrub species such as *S. glauca* and *S. barclayi*.

Shrub Willows

(E) *uŝix̂:* willow bush
   chuyax̂: cane, stick or willow twig

Shrub willows are common on Unalaska and often found in wet areas. They thrive across the flats and valley bottoms, where they sometimes grow into nearly impenetrable tangles. They also favor the river banks and sometimes grow down to the beach. In sheltered spots they grow quite tall with thick trunks, the closest thing the Aleutian Islands have to native trees. Longspurs, sparrows, wrens, and finches sing from their branches

Shrub willow, female catkins

in the spring. In the fall the leaves of some species turn golden yellow and sweet smelling. Winter snows reveal the surrounding tracks of ptarmigan that rely on the buds for food. Stark and beautiful, the dead branches of shrub willows may become wind-gnarled and bleached.

"Willow roses" are the leafy flower-like growths at the tips of some branches. They are supernumerary leaves induced by insects and are often found on the Barclay willow *(Salix barclayi)*. Insects also lay their eggs under the bark of some species, causing swollen galls.

The following key will help separate the three shrub willows found on Unalaska Island. Be aware that some of these species will also grow in a dwarfed or prostrate form in exposed areas.

Also, the key is not foolproof, and once a willow has been separated out it should be studied for the other features that help confirm its identification. The key describes the *mature* leaves, since young leaves are often hairy, but later become hairless. Some of the identifying characteristics appear before the leaves mature: the length of the catkins, whether they are borne on stalks, and if the catkins appear before or with the leaves.

Willow Family / Salicaceae

Key to shrub willows on Unalaska Island:

Choose between A1 and A2.

A1. Under surface of mature leaves densely white, wooly surface not visible. Ovaries densely hairy: See feltleaf willow, *Salix alaxensis.*

A2. Under surface of mature leaves glabrous, or visible through hairs, not densely white and wooly. Ovaries glabrous. Choose between B1 and B2.

B1. Young leaves densely hairy on both surfaces. Mature leaves light green on both surfaces, not shiny, under surface pale green but not glaucous or whitish beneath: See undergreen willow, *Salix commutata.*

Shrub willow, male catkins

B2. Young leaves glabrous or sparsely hairy. Mature leaves glabrous or sparsely hairy on the upper midvein. Upper surface shiny yellow green, under surface glaucous or whitish. See Barclay willow, *Salix barclayi.*

Feltleaf or Alaska Willow
Salix alaxensis (Anderss.) Cov.

LEAVES: elliptic to oblanceolate, 2" to 4" long, margins entire, upper surface dull green, essentially glabrous when mature, under surface tomentose (densely covered with soft creamy white wool or felt).

CATKINS: stalkless, appearing before the leaves, 2" to 4" long at maturity.

SEED CAPSULES: long, pointed, and pubescent (woolly).

The name *alaxensis* comes from an old spelling of Alaska. Only one tall shrub of *S. alaxensis* has been found growing in the town of Unalaska, but it should be watched for since it is found on nearby Unimak Island.

Undergreen or Variable Willow
Salix commutata Bebb

LEAVES: elliptic to obovate, to 2 ½" long, margins entire or glandular toothed, young leaves are densely hairy on both surfaces, older leaves thinly hairy, leaves light green on both surfaces, not shiny, the under surface green or pale but not whitish or glaucous.

STIPULES: persistent, leaf like, to ⅜" long

CATKINS: developing with or after the leaves, ¾" to 1 ½" long.

SEED CAPSULES: ¼" long, hairless, reddish becoming brown with age.

Often grows together with the Barclay willow in sheltered lowlands and valleys and is similar in appearance.

Barclay Willow
Salix barclayi Anderss.

LEAVES: Broadly elliptic to obovate, to 3" long, margins either entire or toothed, especially near the base, leaves pubescent when young, glabrous when older, or pubescent on the upper midvein. Upper surface shiny yellow green, under surface whitish or glaucous. Leaves turn black when drying. Often develops "willow roses."

CATKINS: held on short stalks with two to three leaves, appearing with the leaves, catkins 2" to 3" long.

SEED CAPSULES: short and stout, held on short stalks, villous when young, becoming glabrous, pedicels, ovaries and capsules all glabrous.

Often grows together with the undergreen willow (*S. commutata*) in sheltered lowlands and valleys.

Undergreen willow at left, Barclay willow at right.

Birch Family / *Betulaceae*

Alder
Alnus crispa (Ait.) Pursh
spp. *sinuata* (Regel)
Hult.
(= A. sinuata (Regel) Rydb.)

Alders are a shrub similar to willows. The bark is reddish brown and flecked. The leaf margins are serrated, and the leaves and buds are sticky in the spring. Unlike willows, alders have catkins of both sexes on the same plant. Male catkins are long, shed their pollen and drop. Female catkins are short and upright. After ripening they turn hard and woody, and persist on the branches through the winter.

RANGE:
Western North America and northeastern Asia. In the Aleutians, native only on Unimak Island and introduced to Unalaska and Amaknak (Dutch Harbor).

Buckwheat Family / *Polygonaceae*

Bistort, docks, wild rhubarb, and the sorrels are all familiar members of the buckwheat family. The stems are often jointed; *polygonum* means many knees. The leaves are usually entire (not divided or toothed), their base forming an *ocrea,* or expanded sheath, around the stem. The individual flowers are often very small but so numerous that the whole inflorescence is showy. The three-sided achenes, or single-seeded fruits, are characteristic of the family.

The genus *Rumex* includes what are commonly called the docks and sorrels, the docks generally being the tall-stemmed (to two feet and more) members. They are a confusing group of closely related species, and identification takes a bit of attention. The docks, and especially the sorrels, are highly delicious plants, well worth getting to know.

Sheep Sorrel
Rumex acetosella L.

(E, A) *taangax̂ uqux̂*

Emerging from slender rhizomes, this is a wispy, reddish plant with thin stems usually less than 24" tall. The leaves are glabrous, narrow, and hastate (arrowhead shaped); the blades are oblong to lanceolate with the narrow basal lobes flaring outward. The leaves are mainly clustered near the base of the plant, the lower ones having long petioles, and the upper leaves becoming progressively smaller and having shorter petioles. The flowering stems branch near the top and are covered with a mass of tiny, rusty red flowers.

Sheep sorrel's tender leaves are deliciously tart and are good nibbled raw or tossed into a salad. The Unangan also used the leaves medicinally, steaming and cooling them to place over bruised or irritated skin (Bank 1962). The delicate flowering stems will dry intact for winter bouquets. The plants favor dry stony ground and are often found in dry creek beds and gravel bars or along roadsides.

RANGE:
Northern circumpolar.

Garden or Green Sorrel
Rumex acetosa L.

Emerging from a taproot, the flowering stems are stiff and upright, to 40" tall. The leaves are glabrous, broad, and hastate (arrowhead shaped), the basal lobes pointing back or downward. The lower leaves have long petioles. The upper leaves are attached directly to the flowering stem and become progressively smaller upwards. The branched upper stem bears the numerous tiny, purple-tinged flowers. They later develop into a mass of dangling, reddish green, three-sided seed cases.

Garden sorrel, like the similar but smaller sheep sorrel, has deliciously tart and tender leaves. They are wonderful in salads and eaten raw. Early in the season, before the flowering stems shoot up, the plants create a low circle of leaves. They often grow among other *Rumex* species, favoring damp sites and rocky soil.

RANGE:
Nearly circumpolar and widespread in western Alaska.

Wild Rhubarb, Great Western Dock
Rumex fenestratus Greene
(= *R. occidentalis* Macoun)

(E) *aalungaayax̂;*
  quuguulnaadax̂: sour
(A) *aluungis*

A tall and robust plant emerging from a thick taproot, its stalk is stout, grooved and sectioned, often reddish tinged, and to six feet tall or more. The large ribbed leaves are longer than they are broad and the margins are repand (slightly undulating). The lower leaves are largest, held on long stems, and are often cordate, or heart-shaped, at the base. The leaves become progressively smaller up the stalk. The top branches form a dense, elongated reddish green tassel of small flowers (panicle) which later become a profusion of dangling, three-sided fruits.

Wild rhubarb grows in wet areas and is common along creeksides, springs, and roadside ditches. The stems of young plants are tart and can be peeled and eaten raw or cooked into jams and sauces. Wild rhubarb was also used medicinally by the Unangan. The thin film at the base of the plant was used for bandaging (Hudson 1992). The juice soothed and helped heal chapped lips or lips burned from putchki *(Heracleum lanatum)* juice (N. Galaktianoff, Sr., pers. comm.). Wild rhubarb's soothing attributes were known on the mainland as well, where the mashed leaves were applied to skin irritated by stinging nettles (Scofield 1989). During the winter the dry persistent panicles, bearing a tassel of seeds, provide food for hungry songbirds. *—continues*

RANGE:

R. fenestratus is found throughout the Aleutians and is widespread along the southern Alaska coast and parts of the Interior.

In addition to *Rumex fenestratus,* other species of wild rhubarb, or dock, occur on Unalaska. All members of the genus *Rumex,* they are closely related, similar in appearance, and difficult to distinguish. They are even thought to hybridize. These additional species are described here.

R. arcticus Trautv., arctic dock, ranges throughout arctic Asia and Siberia, and is widespread in Alaska, except in the southern coastal areas. Specimens have been identified, however, from both Unalga and Unalaska islands (ALA Collections). It is very closely related to *R. fenestratus,* and the two are said to hybridize. In typical specimens the leaves of arctic dock are somewhat fleshy and the leaf margins are not distinctly wavy. The base of the leaf is variable, often square or wedge shaped but sometimes cordate (heart shaped). Both the leaves and the flower cluster are often purplish tinged. The fruits are very similar to *R. fenestratus.*

R. longifolius DC. (= *R. domesticus* Hartman), often called garden dock, is said to be an introduced species and not found west of Nikolski (ALA Collections, C. Parker pers. comm.). Its leaves are typically square or rounded at the base and only somewhat reduced in size up the stem. In this species the valves, or flat sides of the fruits, are rounded and broad, often broader then they are long. In both *R. fenestratus* and *R. arcticus,* the valves are ovate to cordate.

R. obtusifolius L., bitter or blunt-leaved dock, is another introduced species (Hultén 1960) that has spread along the southern coastal areas of Alaska. The flowering top is fairly open, with spreading branches, and the flowers are held in distinctive whorls around the stems. The valves, or flat sides of the fruits, are edged with long teeth, and one of the valves has a bright red, raised grain on its surface.

R. transitorius Rech. is an uncommon prostrate-stemmed dock of waste areas and coastal marshes. It is found along coastal western North America, just barely reaching, and rare on, Unalaska.

fruit of
R. fenestratus

fruit of
R. longifolius

fruit and
seed of
R. obtusifolius

Mountain Sorrel, Alpine Sorrel, Sourgrass
Oxyria digyna (L.) Hill

(E) *quugulnaadax̂:* sour

Emerging from a stout rootstock, the flowering stems are glabrous and pale green, 6" to 12" tall. The glabrous, reniform (kidney shaped) leaves are held on long petioles at the base of the plant. The green leaves turn reddish in the fall. The flowers are held in an elongated branched cluster above the basal leaves. The fruits are red, flat, and scale-like, similar to a small version of wild rhubarb.

Mountain sorrel is a hardy plant adapted to life at high elevations. Occasionally, it is found down lower in stony soil and dry stream beds. It can grow up to a foot tall or more in sheltered spots, but in the high tundra and snow patches, it is often dwarfed. Mountain sorrel is one of the few plants that can survive through years when the snow cover does not melt at all during the summer. It is able to stay dormant; the leaves die back, but the over-wintering shoot bud below the ground remains alive (Pielou 1994). The leaves of mountain sorrel are tart, delicious, and high in vitamin C.

RANGE:
Northern circumpolar and widespread across Alaska.

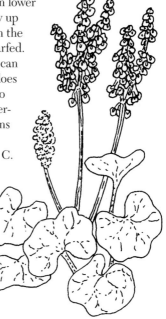

**Bistort, Alpine Bistort,
Viviparous Knotweed,
Ptarmigan Grass**
Polygonum viviparum L.
(= *Bistorta vivipara* (L.)
S. F. Gray)

(E) *chiisuudan:* resembling
fish eggs (the flowering
tops); *quguchuudax̂* (the
edible root); *makaarisax̂*
(from the Russian
makarsha).
(A) *qulunguchiisis*
(A) *tiĝlam aahmaaĝa:* eagle
flower

Emerging from a hard,
thickened, and often twisted rhizome, the single
jointed stems are 4" to 16"
tall. The lower leaves are lanceolate and held on long
petioles, and the upper leaves are smaller, narrower, and sessile. The tiny white to pinkish fragrant
flowers are held in a spike. Beneath the flowers
the upper stem is covered with hard red bulblets
which scatter to become new plants.
Bistort is a common and early bloomer in the
meadows and hillsides. The frilly white
tassel of flowers and the red, egg-shaped
bulblets below them give the plant all of
its descriptive common names. The scientific
name is worth explaining as well: *Polygonum* means
many joints or knees, in reference to the stems, and *viviparum* means to bring forth live young, in reference to
the bulblets. The leaves and roots are edible and the roots
have a faint licorice or almond flavor. The Unangan used
to eat these roots with dried salmon eggs (N. Galaktianoff, Sr., pers. comm.).
RANGE:
Northern circumpolar and widespread in Alaska.

Purslane Family / *Portulacaceae*

Siberian Spring Beauty, Rainflower
Claytonia sibirica L.
(= *Montia sibirica* (L.) Howell.)

(E) *anin. qalngaaĝim luux̂sikangin:* raven's
    spoons.
(A) *qugux̂, qugus. chilum aahmaaĝa:* Lapland
    Longspur flower. *chiĝilĝim aahmaaĝa:*
    marsh flower.

Arising from a slender taproot, the
stems are glabrous and bending, 4" to
20" tall. The stems and leaves are tender and succulent. The leaves are oval
and bluntly pointed, or spoon shaped. The
similarly shaped lower leaves are petiolate,
often withering when the flowers open; the
upper leaves on the flowering stems are sessile
and held in pairs. The plant blooms profusely
with starlike flowers held in open clusters on
long, thin pedicels. The five petals are commonly
either rose pink or white, or sometimes white with pink stripes.
    Spring beauty favors damp ground and grows abundantly in low patches
in open areas as well as shady places, such as under salmonberry *(Rubus*

—continues

spectabilis) bushes. Welcomed very early, the delicious spring greens are sweet and tender and can be eaten raw or steamed. Although it is often the first flower to appear in early May, it has an unusually long blooming period, lasting until September and October. One of the Atkan Aleut names for spring beauty is the Lapland longspur flower. Each spring, just as those songbirds return to the islands, the first spring beauties bloom.

This is also one of two plants known locally as rainflowers; the other rainflower is a member of the buttercup family *(Ranunculus bongardii)*. According to the local saying, if you pick them, you will make it rain.

RANGE:
Western United States, Pacific coast of Alaska, throughout the Aleutian and Commander islands.

OTHER SPECIES:
C. chamissoi; C. perfoliata (introduced); *Montia fontana.*

Ruscus-leaved starwort, Stellaria ruscifolia *Pall. subsp.* aleutica *Hult.*

62

Purslane Family / *Portulacaceae*

Pink or Chickweed Family / *Caryophyllaceae*

Leaves are opposite, simple, and entire (not divided or toothed). Flowers are regular, often small and delicate, usually with five sepals and five petals, and five or ten stamens. The petals are sometimes notched or may be missing altogether. The fruit is a dry capsule.

All the pinks in our area have white flowers, except moss campion, which has rose-pink flowers. All have five petals, except the arctic pearlwort which sometimes has four. The species of *Cerastium* and *Stellaria* may appear to have twice the number since their petals are deeply notched. Other Stellaria species found on Unalaska Island include *S. calycantha* (Ledeb.) Bong. and *S. ruscifolia* Pall. subsp. *aleutica* Hult.

Sitka Starwort, Chickweed
Stellaria sitchana Steud.
(= *S. borealis* Bigelow var. *sitchana* (Steud.) Piper, = *S. borealis* Bigelow var. *bongardiana* (Fern.) Hult.)

Emerging from a rhizome, the stems are thin, branching and fairly upright, to 20" tall. The small, pointed, lanceolate leaves are held in pairs. Flowers are borne on thin stems ascending from the axils of the leaves. The five white petals are very thin, often lacking or inconspicuous between the five longer and broader, pointed sepals. Much variation occurs within this species with respect to flower and leaf size, whether the flowers are borne singly or in branching clusters, and whether the stems have a rough or glabrous surface.

Sitka starwort's flowers look like tiny, delicate, greenish-white stars. It grows in moist places with low, mossy vegetation, such as meadows and along river banks and lake shores. It is often found near willows. Other Stellaria species found on Unalaska Island include the Northern Starwort, *S. calycantha* (Ledeb.) Bong. and the Ruscus-leaved Starwort, *S. ruscifolia* Pall. subsp. aleutica Hult.

RANGE:
Throughout the Aleutians, southern coastal Alaska, and western North America.

Bering Chickweed
Cerastium beeringianum Cham. & Schlecht.

Arising from a taproot and prostrate, rooting stems, the plant forms a spreading mat, with flowering stems ascending 2" to 8" tall. The branching stems bear small lanceolate, dark green leaves and a profusion of delicate white flowers. The small flower's five rounded petals are deeply notched.

Bering chickweed is a lovely plant that often grows in dense clumps along loose cliffs and dry slopes, in beach gravel, and on sandy riverbanks.

RANGE:
Northern circumpolar and widespread in Alaska.

Mouse-Ear Chickweed, Chickweed
Cerastium fontanum Baumg.
(=C. caespitosum, C. vulgatum)

Spindly, branching stems, 4" to 16" tall, grow in loose clumps from weak shallow roots. Both the leaves and stems are grayish green and pubescent. The leaves are oval to lanceolate and held in pairs. The small white flowers are held in loose clusters, arising from the axils of the upper leaves. Flowers have five deeply notched petals and sepals of about the same length. The fruit is a tiny, oblong green capsule; when it dries, it becomes transparent.

Mouse-ear chickweed often grows in the poor rocky soil of roadsides, fields and disturbed areas and is recognized by its grayish green foliage and loose spindly growth.

RANGE:
Northern circumpolar.

OTHER SPECIES:
C. aleuticum Hult.;
C. fischerianum Ser.

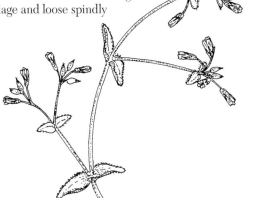

Pink or Chickweed Family / *Caryophyllaceae*

Pearlwort, Arctic Pearlwort
Sagina saginoides (L.) Karst.
(= *S. linnaei* Presl.)

The plant forms a delicate bright green mat with its threadlike stems and very thin leaves. Low growing, it is seldom more than 4" high. The tiny star-like flowers are held on curving stems. The oval green sepals are held widely open and are much longer than the tiny white petals cupped within. The fruit is a tiny, rounded green capsule.

Pearlwort favors open spots, and often grows in the sandy or gravelly soil of river bars and roadsides.

RANGE:
Northern circumpolar.

OTHER SPECIES:
S. intermedia Fenzl.; *S. crassicaulis*
S. Wats.; *S. occidentalis* S. Wats.

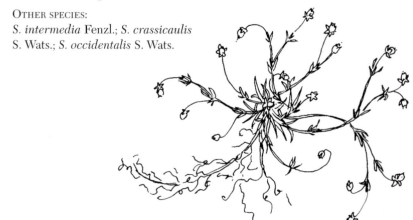

Beach Greens, Scurvy Weed, Seabeach Sandwort
Honckenya peploides (L.) Ehrh.
(= *Arenaria peploides* L.)

(E) *isuĝim aningin:* hair seal's lupine root

A succulent, low-growing, spreading plant with stems that are often many feet long. The stems are often buried in the sand, forming loose mats. The leaves are bright green, thick and fleshy, elliptic to oblong, and pointed. Small greenish-white flowers are held in the axils of the upper leaves. The flowers have five widely spaced white petals and green sepals. Later the plant forms small green pumpkin-shaped pods full of round orange seeds. The seeds begin to sprout in the beach sand in late winter.

Beach greens grow abundantly on sandy and gravel beaches and over sand dunes, often in loose extensive mats. The plant withstands salt spray, and occasionally gets washed over and covered in sand during storms and high tides. The leaves are sweet and tender when young and picked early, although the taste sometimes leaves your mouth a bit dry. They are very nutritious. Early sailors and explorers often suffered miserably from scurvy, a disease resulting from vitamin C deficiency. Once the cause was understood, lemons and limes were carried aboard ship to ward it off, but knowledge of this common coastal plant saved many a sailor from the disease. Vitus Bering and his crew were so sick with scurvy that their expedition was forced to turn back to Kamchatka, but their ship *St. Peter* wrecked on Bering Island. Many, including the captain, did not survive the winter. Georg Wilhelm Steller, the ship's naturalist, fed beach greens to the stranded crew in an attempt to save them. Forty-six survived the terrible winter to spend nine months building a craft from the ship's wreckage, in which they managed to sail back to Russia's Avacha Bay.

seed pods

RANGE:
Northern circumpolar; coastal areas throughout Alaska.

Grove Sandwort, Blunt-Leaved Sandwort
Moehringia lateriflora (L.) Fenzl.
(= *Arenaria lateriflora* L.)

Ascending from rhizomes or stolons, the reddish threadlike stems are 3" to 8" tall. The stems and leaves have a barely visible pubescence. The leaves are lanceolate to oblong, up to 1" long, and held in three to seven opposite pairs. A joint near the tip of the stem bends at an angle, holding the single flower off center. The five oval white petals are two to three times longer than the sepals.

Though widespread in Alaska, this delicate little flower is uncommon here. It blooms in the damp tundra in late July and early August.

RANGE:
Northern circumpolar and widespread throughout Alaska.

Moss Campion, Moss Pink
Silene acaulis L.

This low-growing plant arises from a deep taproot and forms dense mats or cushions. Crowded with tiny, pointed leaves, in bloom the plant becomes a dense cushion of rose pink flowers. The tiny blossoms have very short stems and are held close among the leaves. The flowers have a reddish-purple calyx and five oval petals.

Moss campion is a beautiful, delicate plant that clings to cliffs, rocky places, and waterfall-misted ledges. It blooms very early and sparsely at first; later the cushions are covered with a profusion of tiny flowers, often nearly hiding the leaves.

Like other cushion plants, it stays down out of the wind where its low profile and dense mat of leaves protects it. Selective in habitat and not abundant, it pioneers places inaccessible or too exposed for other plants to take hold. Moss campion spreads very slowly; the plant may take ten years to bloom, and twenty-five years to form a 7" cushion (Zwinger 1972). When hiking and climbing, one should take care not to damage them.

RANGE:
Northern circumpolar, widespread in Alaska, eastern and central Aleutians.

Crowfoot or Buttercup Family / *Ranunculaceae*

A very diverse and well represented family in the Aleutians, this group includes anemones (*Anemone* spp.), buttercups (*Ranunculus* spp.), marsh marigold (*Caltha palustris*) and monkshood (*Aconitum* spp.). All but the marsh marigold and the tiny creeping spearwort have deeply lobed or divided leaves. Many members of the family are highly poisonous. The scientific name *Ranunculus* means "little frog," perhaps because many species live in wet or marshy habitat.

Marsh Marigold, Cowslip
Caltha palustris L.

anim kangaĝa, anim kanaĝa, anim kangaa, anim kangangin: above or on top of the lake

Stems emerge from fibrous roots and root at the nodes. The stems are smooth and hollow, two feet or more long, the longest often reclining and curving upward at the tip. The stems bear smooth, round leaves with shallowly toothed margins. The leaves are commonly about 3" in diameter but sometimes as much as 6". The flowers are bright yellow and consist of a varying number of overlapping sepals; true petals are lacking. Occasionally unusual, dense double flowers form (see photo above). In late summer, the flowers form a head of wrinkled pods which look like tiny cabbages. The pods blacken and dry, spilling their tiny seeds into the moist surroundings.

Marsh marigolds bloom early in springs and wet meadows and along lake shores, sometimes even blooming beneath the surface of the water. The leaves and

—continues

roots are said to be edible only if cooked. An Unangan use was to chew on the root and swallow the juice, which was said to restore strength if one was tired and hungry (Hudson 1977).

RANGE:
Northern circumpolar and throughout the Aleutians.

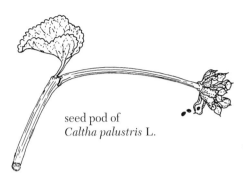

seed pod of
Caltha palustris L.

71

Goldthread, Trifoliate Goldthread
Coptis trifolia (L.) Salisb.
(= *C. trifoliata* (L.) Salisb.)

Named for its long, threadlike, bright yellow underground rhizome. The evergreen leaves are small, stiff, and shiny, and composed of three sharply-toothed leaflets. Flowering stems are 2" to 5" tall. The delicate flowers have five to seven white sepals, which are pinkish on the undersides. The true petals are minute.

Goldthread grows in damp mossy tundra. The long golden rhizome breaks easily; you have to dig down gently into the deep groundcover to unravel it. The Unangan boiled these roots to prepare a medicinal tea (Hudson 1992). The goldthread's flower is similar in size and shape to the starflower *(Trientalis europaea),* but the leaves are quite different; the starflower's leaves are oval shaped and bunched at midstem.

RANGE:
Eastern Asia, throughout the Aleutians, along the Pacific coast into North America.

Monkshood, Mountain or Northern Monkshood, Delphinium-Leaved Monkshood
Aconitum delphinifolium DC.

Emerging from tuberous roots, the stems are stiff and slender and bear a very fine pubescence. The plants stand up to 40" tall, but are usually much shorter. The leaves are palmately lobed (hand-shaped), the lobes cleft nearly to the base. The plants are usually single or few flowered and the blossoms are deep blue and hooded. The flower hood of *A. delphinifolium* is boat shaped, longer than it is high, whereas the hood of *A. maximum* is helmet shaped, higher than it is long.

Mountain monkshood is seldom found near sea level and prefers higher elevations. It is very similar to, but not nearly as common as, the taller monkshood, *A. maximum*. The shorter, more slender stem and the shape of the hood will help identify it. Both species of monkshood are deadly poisonous, especially the tubers.

RANGE:
Eastern Asia and across Alaska.

Aconitum delphinifolium

Aconitum maximum

Monkshood, Kamchatka Aconite
Aconitum maximum Pall.

(E) *aanasnaadam ulaa:* bumblebee's house. *quungdiix̂:* a term also used for the purple orchid *(Orchis aristata).* Both plants were known to be toxic.
(E, A) *maamanuuĝidax̂*
(E) *nuusnuchx̂aadan:* scissors flower, a name also used for the wild iris.

The root is a hard, sometimes round, sometimes irregularly shaped tuber which contains the deadly poison aconitin. The stems are stout and up to seven feet tall. The palmate (hand-shaped) leaves are deeply divided into many segments with prominent veins on the undersides. The plant is topped with numerous deep blue, hooded flowers. The hood on these flowers is helmet-shaped, higher than it is long. As the blossoms drop, the plant forms a cluster of stubby, clawed seed pods.

Monkshood is common in grassy meadows and hillsides, among ferns, putchki *(Heracleum lanatum)* and fireweed *(Epilobium* spp.). These blue-hooded heads nod above the tallest summer grass. The flowers are a favorite sleeping place for bumblebees.

Monkshood is a beautiful but deadly poisonous plant, the root especially so. The poison, aconitum, paralyzes the nerves, and lowers body temperature and blood pressure. The poison may have been used on the harpoon tips of Unangan whale hunters, although this is uncertain. This use was not widely known and may have been kept secret by the whalers (Bank 1962). Extreme caution should be used in handling these plants and in not mistaking them for similar species.

—*continues*

seed pods

Monkshood—*continued*

The cranesbill, *Geranium erianthum,* has very similar leaves, and the lupine, *Lupinus nootkatensis,* has similar flowers. Also, please see the similar but less common mountain monkshood *(A. delphinifolium).*

RANGE:
Kamchatka, Aleutian Islands, Alaska Peninsula.

75

Crowfoot or Buttercup Family / *Ranunculaceae*

Yellow Anemone
Anemone richardsonii Hook.

Emerging from thin, underground rhizomes, the stems are slender, 2" to 8" tall. The leaves are rounded, with shallow lobes and toothed margins. The short-petioled basal leaves emerge along the rhizome, the upper leaves are held in a whorl around the flowering stem. The flowers are solitary, with a varying number of bright yellow overlapping, pointed sepals.

A lovely and uncommon little bloom, the yellow anemone often favors the wet tundra and low vegetation of higher altitudes. It could easily be mistaken for a buttercup, and they are both in the same family.

RANGE:
Eastern Asia, the Aleutians, widespread across Alaska and northern Canada.

May Flower, White Flower, Anemone
Anemone narcissiflora L.

(E) *chix̂udangix̂*
(A) *slukam aahmaag̃a:*
seagull flowers

Stems are up to 24" tall, upright, thick, and villous (covered with silky hairs). The soft leaves are divided into five parts, each part cleft into many rounded lobes. The ivory-white flowers are held in a cluster above the leaves; the six or seven rounded petals overlapping. The pollen-bearing anthers create a bright yellow center. The flowers are very fragrant.

May flowers are a local favorite and one of our first flowers of spring. Pushing up through the old bleached grass of winter, they begin to bloom in mid-May on south-facing hillsides. Long into July, however, after the earlier flowers have bloomed in the foothills, this species can still be found blooming at the higher elevations, where the snowbeds are just melting.

The Atkan Aleut term, seagull flowers, may refer to the soft ivory-white color of the blossoms, or that they bloom just when the gulls are laying their eggs. Although the May flower, like many anemones, is poisonous, the Unangan used its roots for medicinal purposes. A juice extracted by boiling was used to treat hemorrhaging (Hudson 1992).

RANGE:
Northern circumpolar and widespread across Alaska.

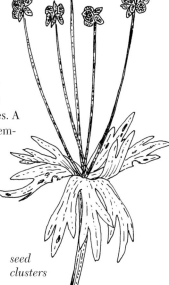

seed clusters

The Buttercups / The Genus *Ranunculus*

The buttercups, or members of the genus ranunculus, can be difficult to identify to species. In trying to tell them apart, it helps to look at the basal or lower leaves; they differ from the upper stem leaves and their shape often helps identify them. Also look at the flattened fruits, called achenes, to see if they have a straight or hooked tip. Some of the bright yellow geum flowers, which are in the rose family, might be mistaken for buttercups, but the buttercups all have glossy petals while geums never do.

White Water Crowfoot
Ranunculus trichophyllus Chaix.
(= *R. aquatilis* L.)

An aquatic plant of shallow water, the stems are long, submerged and branching, to six feet long or more. The submerged leaves are finely divided into thin segments, giving them a feathery appearance underwater. The flowers are white and are either floating on, or held above the surface of, the water. The five white petals do not overlap, and are bright yellow at their base, near the flower's center.

A blooming mass of these floating white flowers in a quiet river bend or slough is a beautiful sight.

RANGE:
Northern circumpolar and widely distributed.

Creeping Spearwort
Ranunculus reptans L.
(=*R. flammula* L.)

This small buttercup has thin, runnerlike stems, arching and rooting in wet ground. Flowers are tiny and fragrant, with five or more bright yellow petals. Leaves are smooth, thin and bright green. Two variations occur: var. *ovalis* has narrowly lanceolate leaves that are much wider than their stems, and var. *filiformis* has leaves so narrow they are scarcely distinguishable from their stems.

It is sometimes found along the edges of a lake or in spots where water has recently receded. It often sends its runners out onto the exposed muddy bottom where a shallow pond has begun to dry up.

RANGE:
Northern circumpolar, widespread in Alaska and throughout the Aleutians.

Eschscholtz Buttercup, Snowbed Buttercup
Ranunculus eschscholtzii Schlecht.

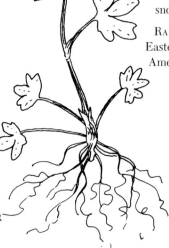

Stems are 4" to 12" tall. Both stems and leaves are glabrous. The lower leaves are highly variable in shape, usually divided into three to five rounded lobes, with each lobe cleft again. The upper leaves are sessile, usually with long undivided lobes. Flowers have five shiny yellow petals which are often variable in size and sometimes shallowly notched. The sepals are half their length.

This small buttercup is fairly uncommon here. It can be found growing in damp meadows or muddy earth where the vegetation is low, often where the snowbeds have melted.

RANGE:
Eastern Asia, across Alaska into western North America, lacking in central Aleutians.

Creeping Buttercup
Ranunculus repens L.

Dark green leaves and flowering stems arise from creeping branches that root at the nodes. The stems are often covered with soft hairs.

The leaves are divided into three leaflets, each leaflet held on a short stem and divided again into three lobes. The flowers have bright, shiny yellow petals, twice the length of the sepals. The sepals are pubescent and not reflexed. The plant forms round heads of small flattened seeds (achenes), and each seed has a short, slightly curved beak.

The creeping buttercup can be distinguished by its thrice-divided leaves and leaflets. It is shorter and leafier than the tall buttercup *(R. acris)*. This species grows wild around the town of Unalaska but is believed to be an introduced species native to Europe.

RANGE:
Northern circumpolar, widespread throughout Alaska.

Buttercup, Common or Tall Buttercup
Ranunculus acris L.
(= *R. acer* L.)

A tall spindly plant, up to 40" high, with thin multibranched stems. The lower leaves are held on long stems, and are deeply divided into three to five parts, each part being cleft again. The upper leaves are sessile, becoming more simple and separating into long lobes. The shiny bright yellow petals overlap, forming a shallow cup. The pubescent sepals are half the length of the petals and are not reflexed (bent backwards). Later the plant forms heads of small flattened seeds, and in this species, the seeds have a short, straight beak.

The tall buttercup is common in grassy fields and meadows, where it often grows among ferns and other tall growth. It is also found in poor soil and disturbed areas.

RANGE:
Northern circumpolar.

Buttercup, Bongard Buttercup, Rainflower
Ranunculus bongardii
E. Greene
(= *R. uncinatus* D. Don)

(E) *chix̂tadan, chix̂tam chix̂uudngii, chix̂tam chiĝuudngii:* rain flower
(A) *chix̂talix, chix̂tam aahmaaĝii:* rain flower
(A) *qanglaaĝim aahmaĝii:* rainflower (species uncertain)

Stems are stout, densely covered with soft hairs, and usually less than 32" tall. This species is generally shorter than the tall buttercup *(R. acris)*. The basal leaves are broader, not as deeply cleft and tend to get brown markings or dark blotches with age. The petals are bright yellow. The flowers tend to be more flattened and not as cupped as *R. acris*. The pubescent sepals under the petals are reflexed (bent backwards). The plant forms heads of small flattened seeds which have long, hooked beaks.

This is one of the plants known locally as the rainflower, depending on whom you ask. Locals say if you pick these flowers, you will make it rain. Perhaps this derives from an old Unangan legend that refers to the plant's being used as a poison. Slipped into food, the juice of the buttercup was said to make a well man take sick and 'dry up' into nothing. But constant gathering of the buttercup was dangerous; it would bring on bad rainstorms and drown the wrongdoer at sea (Banks 1962).

RANGE:
Pacific Northwest, southern coastal Alaska, into the Aleutians.

OTHER SPECIES:
R. sulphureus Soland.;
R. occidentalis Nutt.

Meadow Rue
Thalictrum minus L. ssp.
   kemense (E. Fries) Hult.
(= *T. kemense* E. Fries.,
   T. hultenii B. Boivin.)

An upright leafy plant with smooth, slender branching stems, 12" to 40" tall. The leaves are delicately divided and held in three small, rounded leaflets, each leaflet having one to three shallow lobes. The buds are pinkish, the flowers small and inconspicuous, clustered among the leaves. They are most visible in maturity when the yellow anthers are hanging from their long filaments.

Tall and leafy meadow rue has a delicate appearance in the way it holds its leaves. The plants are wind pollinated, and the dangling tassels are well designed for this. It is found in scattered locations on hillsides and in valleys and meadows, often among ferns and other tall growth.

RANGE:
Widespread in northern Eurasia; the only populations found in America are isolated in the eastern Aleutians and in interior Alaska.

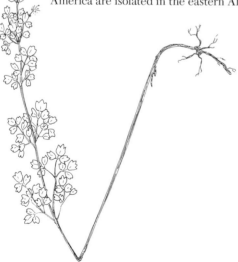

Poppy Family / *Papaveraceae*

Alaska Poppy
Papaver alaskanum Hult.

A lovely low-growing wildflower arising from a dense clump of finely lobed leaves. The long curving to upright stems bear single showy flowers, with four pale yellow petals, later developing into cylindrical seed capsules. Poppies are scarce in our area, but can be found along gravel river beds in Unalaska Valley and occasionally on the cliff faces.

RANGE:
Asia and Alaska

Mustard Family / *Cruciferae or Brassicaceae*

Members of the mustard family are distinguished by their alternate leaves and regular flowers bearing four petals, four sepals and six stamens. Of the six stamens, four are longer than the other two. This design is specific to the mustards, so it is easy to recognize members of the family. Identification at the species level however, can be perplexing. Species can be highly variable, especially in the shape of their leaves. The fascinating mature seed pods or fruits of the mustards are often what identify the plants. The shapes vary from long thin bristles to oval or heart-shaped pods. If these fruits are *more* than twice as long as they are wide, they are called siliques. If they are *less* than twice as long as wide, they are known as silicles. Each fruit is divided into two sections separated by a thin wall. The fruits become dry and split open at maturity. Often the stalks elongate when the fruits are developing, perhaps to release the seeds in the wind. The flowers are held in spikes or racemes. Many species are coastal or prefer dry and rocky soil. The mustards include many familiar vegetables, such as kale, cabbage, and bok choy, so it is not surprising that the family offers some tasty wild greens as well.

Spoonwort, Scurvy Weed
Cochlearia officinalis L.

Emerging from taproots, the plant forms loose, low-growing clumps. The stems and leaves are glabrous and succulent. The spoon-shaped basal leaves are held on long petioles. The flowering stem leaves are sessile, more rounded or wedge shaped, and usually somewhat toothed. The small flowers, held in dense clusters, have white petals and yellow centers. After flowering, the plant forms long stalks bearing small oblong to rounded seed pods. The pale dry stalks of the previous winter are often still present through the summer.

Spoonwort prefers coastal areas, thriving in rocky soil and crevices. The leaves are high in vitamin C and were known as a cure for scurvy. The leaves can be eaten either raw or steamed.

RANGE:
Northern circumpolar and widespread along the Alaska coast.

Winter Cress, Yellow Rocket
Barbarea orthoceras
Ledeb.

Emerging from a tap-root, the stems are stout and smooth, often purple-tinged, and up to 40" tall. The leaves are smooth and dark purplish green; the lower leaves are lyre-shaped with large terminal lobes, the upper leaves are coarsely toothed and lobed. The small yellow flowers are held in clusters. As the plant matures and the flowers drop, long narrow pods, or siliques, form like bristles along the upper stem.

Winter cress is a tall and ragged-looking plant, sometimes waist to shoulder high. It is common along the roadsides and in dry areas, often growing near the coast among artemisia (*Artemesia* spp.) and fireweed (*Epilobium* spp.).

RANGE:
Northern circumpolar and widespread in Alaska.

Siliques form as the plant matures.

Umbel-Flowered
Bitter Cress
Cardamine umbellata
E. Greene
(= *C. oligosperma* Nutt.)

Arising from taproots, the stems are smooth and often curving, 4" to 20" tall. The leaves are variable. The lower leaves consist of pairs of small, broad and rounded leaflets, ending in a larger leaflet at the tip. The upper leaves are lanceolate. The flower cluster resembles an umbel, the pedicels almost radiating from a common point. The petals are white and rounded, less than ¼" long. The thin pods, or siliques, are less than an inch in length.

Bitter cress grows in damp places, in sandy or poor soil, sometimes near the beach. The tiny white flowers bloom very early in the spring. It can be hard to distinguish from another Unalaska species, the cuckoo flower, *C. pratensis*, whose flowers are slightly larger and upper leaves more linear. The young leaves of both plants make edible and tasty greens.

RANGE:
Eastern Asia, Alaska, Yukon, Pacific Northwest.

OTHER SPECIES:
Cardamine bellidifolia L., *C. pratensis* L.

Mustard Family / *Cruciferae or Brassicaceae*

Draba, Northern Rock Cress
Draba borealis DC.
(= *Draba unalaschcensis* DC.)

The stems are single or branching from the base, slender and often curving, 2" to 12" tall. They are covered with fine branched hairs. The basal leaves are clustered and oblong to lance shaped. The one or more stem leaves are widely spaced and often shallowly toothed. The flowers are white, with four shallowly notched petals, and held in a crowded cluster at the top of the stems. As the plant matures the stems elongate, and flat lance-shaped pods, or silicles, develop. They later twist into spirals to throw out their seeds.

Northern rock cress is common throughout the Aleutians, and is often found growing in dry or rocky soil.

RANGE:
Eastern Asia and Alaska.

Cliff Hanger
Draba hyperborea (L.) Desv.
(= *D. grandis* DC.)

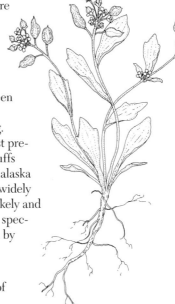

This mustard is a low-growing plant with flowering stems 4" to 14" tall. The basal leaves are held in a loose tuft. They are smooth and bright green, 4" to 6" long, with three to five lobes and widely spaced teeth. The stem leaves are smaller and short-stemmed or sessile. The flowering stems curve upward and recline with length. They branch at the top and the small flowers are held in a cluster above the leaves. The flowers have four yellow petals and green sepals. After flowering the plant forms smooth elliptic pods up to an inch long.

Aptly named, cliff hanger has a most precarious niche, clinging to sea-swept bluffs along the coast. It is uncommon on Unalaska and populations of the plant are often widely spaced. How the plant finds these unlikely and nearly inaccessible spots has led me to speculate on whether the seeds are carried by the surf as well as the wind.

RANGE:
Eastern Asia, Aleutians, Pacific coast of Alaska.

Kamchatka Rock Cress
Arabis lyrata L. ssp. *kamchatica* (Fisch.) Hult.
(= *A. Kamchatica* Fisch.)

Emerging from a taproot, the stems are up to 16" tall, branching near the base of the plant. Both the stems and leaves are smooth. The basal leaves, held in a rosette, are lyre shaped and lobed, tapering to slender petioles. The stem leaves are shorter, nearly sessile, the lower ones remotely lobed or toothed, the uppermost lance shaped to linear. The flowers are small and loosely bunched at the top of the stems, with four white to pinkish, rounded petals. The seed pods, or siliques, are very thin and up to 1 ½" long.

Kamchatka rock cress grows in sandy or stony soil, often near the coast. The young leaves have a delicious radish flavor and can be eaten raw or steamed.

RANGE:
Eastern Asia, Alaska, Yukon, and southward to western North America.

Rock Cress, Hairy
Rock Cress
Arabis hirsuta (L.) Scop.
spp. *eschscholtziana*
(Andrz.) Hult.

Emerging from a taproot, the single stems are
8" to 24" tall and often reddish tinged. Both
the leaves and stems are densely hirsute. The
basal leaves are oblong to lance shaped, roughly
toothed, and form a flat rosette. The stem leaves
are alternate and become narrower the higher
they grow on the stem. The small white flowers
are held in a top cluster, with four rounded petals
about ¼" long. The unopened buds are reddish.
The seed pods, or siliques, are smooth, erect and
very thin, 1" to 3" long.

Rock cress grows in dry, sandy or rocky soil and is
often found along roadsides. Its species name, *hirsuta,*
means bearing coarse or stiff hairs, and the lower stems especially can be quite hairy.

RANGE:
Western North America, southern Alaska to the eastern Aleutians.

Sundew Family / *Droseraceae*

**Sundew,
Round-Leaved
Sundew**
Drosera rotundifolia L.

A very low-growing plant in which the basal leaves form dense rosettes. The upper sides of the tiny, round, yellow green leaves are fringed and colored by delicate red glandular hairs. The sticky fluid produced by the glands traps tiny insects that the plant digests. The slender curling flower stems rise above the leaves and are up to 4" tall. The tips unfold a row of tiny flowers with five white petals.

The sundew is a curious-looking plant of wet meadows and bogs, where the tiny red-fringed leaves are an eye-catching feature. Sundew grows among creeping spearwort *(Ranunculus reptans)*, bog cranberry *(Oxycoccus microcarpus)*, and butterwort *(Pinguicula vulgaris)*, often on wet mossy mounds.

RANGE:
Northern circumpolar and widespread in Alaska.

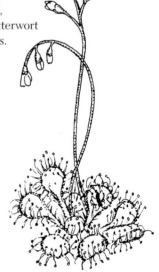

Saxifrage Family / *Saxifragaceae*

The name of this family comes from the Latin *saxum* (rock) and *frangere* (to break), since many species inhabit rocky slopes and cliffs. The saxifrages are herbaceous plants, with leaves varying in shape but often mostly basal. The flowers are regular and all have five sepals, five petals and five or ten stamens. Many develop the characteristic double-beaked fruit. An exception is the grass-of-parnassus *(Parnassia kotzebuei)*, with fruit that is a one-celled capsule. Most saxifrages in the Aleutians are small, low-growing plants. Purple mountain *(Saxifraga oppositifolia)*, bracted *(S. bracteata)* and tufted saxifrages *(S. caespitosa)* are true cliff dwellers, brightening the rocky faces and ledges. The thyme-leaved saxifrage *(S. serpyllifolia)* is only found at high elevations, has tiny bright yellow flowers and is very scarce. The brook saxifrage *(S. punctata)* prefers gravel river bars and damp scree slopes. The leather-leaved *(Leptarrhena pyrolifolia)* is the tallest Aleutian species, preferring wet meadows, while the little grass-of-parnassus favors drier open spots.

Cliff faces such as this are favored by many Saxifrage species.

Leather-Leaved Saxifrage
Leptarrhena pyrolifolia
(D. Don) Ser.

(E, A) *alix̂siisix̂*

Emerging from a thick, horizontal rootstock, the stems are dark red, upright and 8" to 14" tall. At the base of the stem is a mat of shiny, dark green leaves, often with dead leaves persisting underneath. The leaves are ovate to oblong, leathery, and have serrate margins. In early summer the stems bear a cluster of small, inconspicuous white flowers. These later develop into unusual branching, coral-like tops with dark red, double-beaked fruits. This double-beaked fruit is characteristic of saxifrages. (A rarely seen form, shown on the previous page, has pale yellow-green stems and fruits.)

Leather-leaved saxifrage prefers wet ground, seeps and stony pond edges, and often grows in patches. By fall, the stiff stems and branched tops turn cinnamon brown and dry intact. They are interesting to collect and make unusual bouquets. The leaves of this saxifrage stay green long into winter. The Unangan made a medicinal tea from these leaves, which was used to treat sicknesses such as influenza (Bank 1962).

RANGE:
Aleutians, Pacific coast of Alaska, into western Canada and the Pacific Northwest.

Purple Mountain Saxifrage
Saxifraga oppositifolia L.

Plants form a compact mat of crowded, branching stems densely covered with very small leaves. The leaves are about ¼" long, ovate, and fringed with stiff hairs. Held opposite each other, they overlap like scales in four rows along the stems. The showy flowers are purple and held singly on the stem tips. The five rounded petals are about ⅜" long. In full bloom the flowers nearly cover the mat of leaves.

Purple mountain saxifrage is an exceptionally early bloomer, the bright purple flowers appearing at the end of April or the first week of May. Only some of the heath plants bloom earlier. Getting a close look at them, however, can be risky, as they cling to wet, rocky crevices, and steep cliffs.

This plant is superficially like moss campion *(Silene acaulis),* another tufted plant that favors the same habitat, but moss campion leaves are narrow and flat, the flowers are smaller with pink petals, and they bloom later in the season.

RANGE:
This plant is quite rare on Unalaska. This is a circumpolar species that extends into the Aleutian Islands from both the east and the west. It has not been recorded in the central islands, where there seems to be a gap in its range.

Brook Saxifrage, Cordate-Leaved Saxifrage
Saxifraga punctata L.

Flowering stems are long and slender, 4" to 20" tall, often reddish and covered with fine hairs. The basal leaves are held below on shorter petioles. The leaves are roughly circular in outline and scalloped with rounded teeth. This is a highly variable species. The leaves may be glabrous or pubescent. They may be thick and fleshy or they may be thin. They may or may not be edged in red. The flowers are white, small, and numerous. The petals are ovate, and the fruit is a dark reddish purple, double-beaked capsule. The flowers may be held in a dense, rounded cluster at the top of the stem (as shown in the photo), or they may be held in a loose panicle, the flowering stem being branched and branched again (as shown in the sketch).

Five subspecies of *S. punctata* L.—*nelsoniana, insularis, pacifica, porsildiana*, and *charlottae*—are described in Eric Hultén's *Flora of Alaska and Neighboring Territories* (1968). Hultén describes three subspecies of *S. punctata* reaching the Aleutians.

The brook saxifrage is a lovely and fairly common flower here. It grows in wet and gravelly spots, along stream bars and damp slopes. The young leaves are a widely used traditional green food and are high in vitamins.

Range:
Widespread throughout Alaska.

Bracted Saxifrage
Saxifraga bracteata
    D. Don
    (= S. *rivularis* var. *lauren-*
      tiana (Ser.) Engler.)

A low-growing saxifrage; the plants are 1" to 8" tall. The small, glabrous green leaves are held on thin branching petioles, and crowded beneath the flowers. The leaves are reniform (kidney-shaped) and broader than they are long, with five to seven lobes, or very rounded teeth. The white flowers have five oval-shaped, widely spaced petals and the green sepals are half their length.

A coastal dweller, bracted saxifrage favors moist, lichen-covered ledges and is often found in small clumps wedged into rocky crevices.

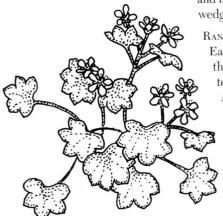

RANGE:
    Eastern Asia, Bering Strait, throughout the Aleutians, scattered along the Pacific coast of Alaska.

Tufted Saxifrage
Saxifraga caespitosa L.

Flowering stems are 2" to 6" tall, arising from a dense mat of overlapping, tufted, green leaves. These small basal leaves are flabellate (fan-shaped) and tipped with three to five lobes. A few smaller and narrower leaves are held on the thin reddish-green flowering stems. The stems branch at the top to hold one to three small, white, bell-shaped flowers. The five oblong petals are twice as long as the reddish sepals.

By September the petals have dropped and the stems dry stiff. The basal leaves form into numerous tight rosettes of leaves, each cluster looking like a tiny cabbage. During the winter the dead, dry outer leaves protect the green tufts within. The new leaves are tightly curled and awaiting spring.

Tufted saxifrage favors stony, mossy spots, from the coastal cliffs to high in the mountains.

RANGE:
Northern circumpolar, only in the eastern Aleutians.

Grass-of-Parnassus
Parnassia kotzebuei
Cham. & Schlecht.

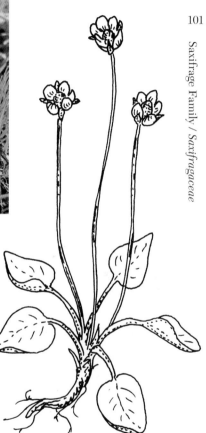

Emerging from short rhizomes, the leaf-less stems are slender, glabrous, and 2" to 6" tall. The stems arise from a rosette of spoon-shaped basal leaves. Each stem bears a single flower at its top. The five small white petals are oblong and no longer than the green sepals. The flowers later develop into wrinkled, cone-shaped capsules.

Grass-of-parnassus grows where the vegetation is low, often in mossy ground, and in disturbed areas.

RANGE:
Widespread in Alaska and the Yukon, and found throughout the Aleutians.

Rose Family / *Rosaceae*

Among the roses are some of our favorite flowers and berries; the bright yellow *Potentilla* spp. and *Geum* spp., the fragrant burnet *(Sanguisorba stipulata)*, the salmonberries *(Rubus spectabilis)*, nagoon berries *(Rubus arcticus)*, and wild strawberries *(Fragaria chiloensis)*. Most have showy flowers that are pollinated by insects, and in the Unalaska area all have five petals, except the burnet, which has none. The leaves are highly variable and often striking. The family includes both woody and herbaceous plants which range in size from the tall salmonberry bushes to the tiny low-growing sibbaldia *(Sibbaldia procumbens)*. This is a large and diverse family, well represented in Alaska and found throughout the world. Species have come into the Aleutians from both Asia and North America. Both salmonberries and burnet have come across mainland Alaska but have reached no farther west than the eastern Aleutians. Wild strawberries followed the same path but reached the central islands. Most of the geums extend throughout the chain. Marsh fivefinger *(Potentilla palustris)* is circumpolar and is migrating into the islands from both directions but has yet to meet in the middle. In the westernmost Aleutians, an Asian species of mountain ash *(Sorbus sambucifolia)* occurs.

Nagoon Berry
Rubus arcticus L. ssp. *stellatus* (Sm.) Boiv.
(= *R. stellatus* Smith)

*aahmaadax̂, hamax̂, haamachiiyax̂,
    aamchiiyax̂*

A low-growing plant with stems 2" to 7" tall, the
nagoon berry emerges from a woody rootstock.
The leaves are deeply rugose (wrinkled), serrated,
and divided into three blunt lobes. They are similar to
the salmonberry's leaf but are smaller and more rounded.
The rose pink petals are long, narrow, and pointed. The
dark red sepals between them are shorter and also pointed.
The plant bears a single, shiny, bright ruby-red berry with large druplets.

The exquisite taste of nagoon berries have earned them the reputation
as the jewels of all Alaska berries; a small
jar of jelly is said to fetch an extraordinary
price. But nature offers them sparingly;
they seldom fruit in abundance and grow
in scattered patches. They favor mossy
meadows and semi-dry tundra where
the vegetation is low, sometimes growing
among reindeer lichen (*Cladonia* spp.).

RANGE:
Throughout the Aleutians and widespread in Alaska. The species as a whole
is circumpolar.

104

Salmonberry
Malina bushes (from the Russian)
Rubus spectabilis Pursh

alagnax̂, halagnax̂, alagnam ingiiga

A tall bush with long, thin and straight woody stems that form dense thickets, often reaching well overhead. The stems are sometimes prickly near the base. The leaves are large, coarsely serrated and divided into three leaflets. Flowers are rose pink; the five pointed petals are often wrinkled, and the calyx sits behind them like a green cap. The sweet and juicy berries vary in color from orange red to purple and are often as big as a walnut.

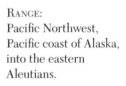

Salmonberries grow in abundance in Unalaska's hills and ravines. The flowers bloom early in the spring and are a favorite of the bumblebees. The berries, picked by the bucketful, are excellent eaten fresh or made into pies, jams, and jellies. Freezing them on baking sheets before putting them into bags prevents them from squashing.

RANGE:
Pacific Northwest,
Pacific coast of Alaska,
into the eastern
Aleutians.

Wild Strawberry, Beach Strawberry
Fragaria chiloensis (L.) Duchesne

(E) *tudungax̂, tudungux̂, atudungax̂*
(A) *tudunam tanasinin, tuzaangux̂*

A low-growing plant with long, red runners, this strawberry has stems covered with long, silky hairs. The leaves are divided into three coarsely serrated leaflets, which are shiny green above, pale and silky underneath. The flowers have five white, rounded petals and yellow centers. The fruit is a small but very sweet, bright red berry.

Finding a patch of wild strawberries while out hiking is a noteworthy delight, since they are not nearly as common as our other berries. Known locations tend to become well-kept secrets. The trailing plants favor areas of low vegetation, such as dry tundra and occasional roadside spots.

RANGE:
Pacific Northwest, Pacific coast of Alaska, into the central Aleutians.

Marsh Fivefinger, Purple or Marsh Cinquefoil
Potentilla palustris (L.) Scop.
(= *Comarum palustre* L.)

Ascending from woody rhizomes, the stems are slender and usually less than 24" tall. The leaves are divided into five sharply serrated leaflets, hence the name fivefinger. The leaves are dark green above and pale beneath. The flowers are unusual; both the long pointed sepals and the much shorter petals are dark purplish brown. The unopened flowers look like rosebuds. Lovely and uncommon, the purple cinquefoil grows in the marshy ground of wet meadows and along river banks; the scientific name *palustris* means "of the marsh." At first glance, its dark appearance may make it seem to be a dried plant. The purple flowers are unique in the genus *Potentilla,* since all the other species have yellow flowers.

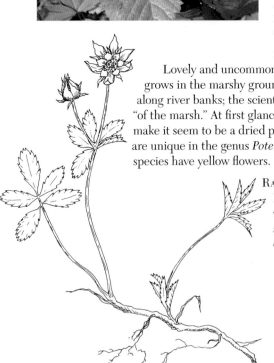

RANGE:
Northern circumpolar and widespread in Alaska, but apparently lacking in the central Aleutian Islands.

Cinquefoil
Potentilla villosa Pall.

Emerging from a stout, woody perennial base, the plant forms a dense, low-growing tuft of leaves. The flowering stems are often very short and seldom more than 10" tall in sheltered spots. The stems, leaves, and sepals are villous. The leaves are grayish green above, silvery tomentose underneath, and divided into three coarsely toothed leaflets, very similar to a strawberry leaf. The flowers are bright yellow, the petals turning deeper yellow, sometimes almost orange, at their base. The five to seven petals are broad and shallowly notched, often overlapping.

By late winter or early spring, when spears of new grass are just poking up along the rocky beaches, tufts of old, dry cinquefoil leaves can be found in cliff crevices. They look quite dead, but already tucked inside are new green leaves. Cinquefoils cling to lichen-covered rocks, ledges and cliffs along the beach. Though mainly coastal, they also grow in dry rocky soil farther inland.

Note: While the bright yellow flowers of the *Geums* and *Potentillas* are similar, attention to their leaves and their habitat will help in distinguishing them.

RANGE:
Pacific Northwest, Alaska, throughout the Aleutians, into Eastern Asia.

Silverweed, Pacific Silverweed, Wild Sweet Potato
Potentilla egedii Wormsk. ssp. *grandis* (Torr. & Gray) Hult.
(=*P. pacifica* How., *P. anserina* L. in part)

taangam daĝdaluu, taangam daĝdaluga, taangam dax̂daluu: water stopper, plant that detains water, can't wet in water, from *taangax̂:* water, and *dax̂talix:* to stop

Rooting from long reddish runners, the plants often spread into large patches. The long-petioled and bending leaves are composed of pairs of oblong, sharply toothed leaflets, which are shiny green above, pale, and villous underneath. The lowermost leaflets are smallest, becoming larger toward the tip, the terminal leaflet up to 2" long. Between them, very tiny leaflets appear. The flowering stems are leafless and slender, to 12" or more long. The flowers are bright yellow, the oval petals widely spaced and not overlapping.

Silverweed roots in damp ground along seashores and in marshes near the beach. Older plants develop a long, fleshy, sweet-tasting root. In the spicy-scented marshes of fall, the silverweed's beautiful bending leaves turn flaming orange and yellow.

RANGE:
The species as a whole is northern circumpolar and widespread in the Pacific Northwest, Alaska, and eastern Asia. Lacking in the central Aleutian Islands.

Sibbaldia
Sibbaldia procumbens L.

A low-growing plant with woody perennial stems forming mats. The small leaves, held on reddish petioles, are divided into three wedge-shaped (cuneate) leaflets, each tipped with three teeth. The stems and leaves are pubescent. The flowering stems, to 4" tall, are crowded with tiny yellow star-like flowers; the five widely spaced petals are shorter than the surrounding sepals.

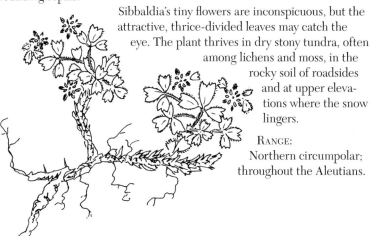

Sibbaldia's tiny flowers are inconspicuous, but the attractive, thrice-divided leaves may catch the eye. The plant thrives in dry stony tundra, often among lichens and moss, in the rocky soil of roadsides and at upper elevations where the snow lingers.

RANGE:
Northern circumpolar; throughout the Aleutians.

Large-Leaved Avens
Geum macrophyllum Willd.

Emerging from a thick, woody base, the stems
are stout, leafy, hispid (with firm stiff hairs), and
up to 40" tall. The lower leaves have long petioles
and consist of numerous leaflets in opposite
pairs, the smallest leaflets being toward the
base, becoming larger and ending in a very
large, three-lobed leaflet. The upper
leaves, bunched at the top under the
flowers, are large and broad, coarsely
and unevenly toothed. The leaves are
hispid on both surfaces, which gives
them a dry feel. The small yellow flowers
are held in a cluster among the upper leaves.
The five widely spaced petals do not overlap.
The green sepals bend backwards as the plant matures, and are as long or longer than the petals. The
flower's center is greenish and later forms a large round,
bristly cluster of tiny fruits (achenes).

Large-leaved avens grow in meadows, fields, and roadsides, often in
disturbed areas. A mat of old leaves persists on the ground throughout the
winter, among which green leaves are also present. They seem able to continue growing, on and off, through intermittent freezes and thaws.

RANGE:
Widespread in south coastal Alaska and throughout the Aleutians.

Avens
Geum calthifolium
Menzies

(E) *hamidux̂, amidux̂*
(A) *hamidug̈ix̂*

Emerging from a stout, woody perennial base, the stems are reddish, pubescent, slender, and often bending, 4" to 12" tall. The leaves are rounded and deeply rugose, pubescent (fuzzy) on both sides, and the margins are crenate. The basal leaves have long petioles; the upper leaves encircle the stem below the bright yellow flowers. The five broad petals barely overlap, and are twice as long as the sepals.

Common in meadows and hillsides, avens often grow among yarrow *(Achillea borealis),* and in dwarf dogwood *(Cornus* spp.) and crowberry heath. The Unangan used this plant's leaves and roots medicinally. A tea boiled from the roots was used as a tonic for sore throats and colds. Leaves, boiled and wet, were used as a poultice over a wound to help healing (Bank 1962). Another method involved singeing the leaves over a fire to remove the short hairs, rubbing fox oil onto the burned side and binding the leaf over a wound with a cloth (Hudson 1992).

In the Aleutians, the ranges of *Geum calthifolium* and *Geum rossii* overlap, and a hybrid between the two can be found. Described as *Geum x macranthum* (Kearney) B. Boi. (= *G. calthifolium x rossii*), it shares features of both plants; the leaves especially look like a cross between the two (Hultén 1960). Please see the accompanying photo and drawing.

Geum x macranthum

RANGE:
Pacific coast of Alaska, the Aleutians, eastern Asia.

Ross Avens
Geum rossii (R. Br.) Ser.
(= *Acomastylis rossii* (R. Br.) Greene)

Emerging from a stout, woody perennial base, the leafy green stems are 3" to 12" tall. The long, smooth basal leaves are divided into many, often overlapping, lobed leaflets. The flowering stems bear reduced leaves just beneath the large, bright yellow flowers. The petals are rounded and overlapping, about ½" long and broad.

An alluring plant with long, dark, fern-like leaves, Ross avens is found only at upper elevations in dry stony tundra and snow beds. It often grows among lousewort (*Pedicularis* spp.) and lagotis (*Lagotis glauca*). Here in the Aleutians, plants that are a hybrid of this species and *Geum calthifolium* can be found, and the leaves especially bear characteristics of both. The cross is known as *Geum X macranthum* and is described under *G. calthifolium*.

RANGE:
Widespread in Alaska, throughout the Aleutians, into eastern Asia.

OTHER SPECIES:
Found in wet meadows, but very scarce here, is *Geum pentapetalum* (L.) Makino, previously known only in the central Aleutians, Japan and eastern Siberia. The petals are white.

Low avens, Geum pentapetalum *(L.) Makino.*

Burnet, Sitka Great Burnet
Sanguisorba stipulata Raf.
(= S. sitchensis C. A. Mey.*)*

Emerging from a thick rootstock, the long and bending leaves are composed of numerous pairs of sharply serrated, oblong leaflets. The young
leaflets are often folded. The upright flowering stems are
8" to 32" tall and topped with a dense, elongate spike of
small apetalous flowers. Most noticeable are the long
white filaments.

In bloom, burnet looks like a frilly white
bottle-brush. The flowers are very fragrant. The name *Sanguisorba* means to
absorb or staunch blood; the leaves and
especially the roots are highly astringent.
A tea brewed from the leaves is reputedly
a good tonic, and the young leaves are edible.
Burnet favors meadows, marshes, and wet hillsides
and often grows among yarrow *(Achillea borealis),* fleabane *(Erigeron peregrinus),* and pyrola
(Pyrola spp.).

RANGE:
Widespread in the Pacific Northwest, Alaska, eastern
Asia. Lacking in the central and western Aleutians.

Pea Family / *Leguminosae* or *Fabaceae*

Lupine
Lupinus nootkatensis Donn.

(E) *tanĝaĝim aningin*: bear roots
(A) *ahnix̂*: root; *tanam asxuu*: the land's nail or spike

Arising from a long and woody root, the stems are stout and 8" to 40" tall. The leaves are composed of oblong leaflets which fan out radially. The stems bear long full spikes of blue flowers; each is deepest blue purple at the base, turning lighter purple, and tipped with white. By late August the seed pods form. These two-inch pubescent pods turn black and will rattle when shaken in the hand. When dry, the pods twist open quickly and throw out their hard, speckled, bean-like seeds.

Although the Unangan used the lupine's long roots for food, the seeds

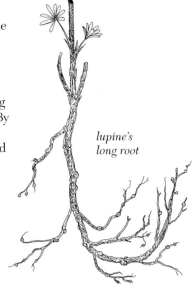

lupine's long root

are said to be poisonous (Hultén 1968). Also, be certain not to mistake this plant for the monkshood (*Aconitum* spp.), which has somewhat similar flowers and a poisonous root. The shape of the leaves will help distinguish the two. Lupines often grow in stands on dry slopes, in gravel and sandy places, and along cliffs and coastal areas. Color variation occurs within the species, and in among a stand of deep blue lupine, one occasionally finds plants with white, pink, or violet purple flowers. After a rain the palmate leaves hold prismatic water droplets at their centers.

RANGE:
Throughout the Aleutians, the southern half of Alaska (mainly coastal) into British Columbia.

115

Pea Family / *Leguminosae* or *Fabaceae*

seed pods

Beach Pea, Sweet Pea, Vetch
Lathyrus maritimus L. ssp. *pubescens* (Hartm.) C. Regel
(= *L. japonicus* Willd. var. *aleuticus* (Greene) Fern.

(E) *kuumĝuх̂*
(A) *chugum aahmaaĝii:* sand flower

Emerging from slender rhizomes, the
low bending vines are 4" to 24" long,
and tipped with curling tendrils. The
leaflets are smooth, oval to broadly
elliptic in shape and held in pairs. The
vines are branching, and
clasping the joints are broad,
leaf-like stipules, up to 1 ½" long. The winged
rose-purple flowers are showy and held in loose
clusters. By late August the blossoms drop and
long, green pods begin to form.
The blossoms of the beach pea bejewel the sandy
shores and dunes where it thrives. The clambering
vines sometimes cover large areas. The beach pea is not
widely used as an edi-
ble plant. Though some
references say the pods
are edible, a number of
pea species contain cu-
mulative toxins (Scofield 1989).

RANGE:
Northern circumpolar, coastal,
throughout the Aleutians.

Wild Pea, Vetchling
Lathyrus palustris L. ssp. *pilosus* (Cham.) Hult.

Emerging from slender rhizomes, the vines are bending but
fairly upright, 16" to 40" long, and tipped with curling, usually
branching tendrils. The leaflets are smooth,
lance shaped to linear and held in pairs.
The vines are branching, and at the joints
are a pair of small, pointed, winglike
stipules. The winged, rose purple flowers are held in a loose cluster.

The wild pea is very similar to the
beach pea *(L. maritimus)*, but is recognized by the narrower leaflets, winglike
stipules and more upright growth also.
It is not as profuse a bloomer as the beach
pea, having fewer and smaller flowers.
Usually found a bit more inland and
back from the beach, the wild pea grows
in wet meadows and along riverbanks,
often among the willows *(Salix* spp.),
fireweed *(Epilobium* spp.), and grasses
(Gramineae).

RANGE:
Northern circumpolar, throughout the
Aleutians.

Geranium Family / *Geraniaceae*

Cranesbill,
  Wild Geranium
Geranium erianthum DC.

(E) *anisnaadam*
  (*aanisnaadax̂:* bumble
  bee)
(E, A) *chunusix̂,*
  chuhnusix̂: an awl or
  tool for stabbing, also a
  pricker, sculpin spine,
  mosquito mouth, or fish
  spear (in reference to
  the flower's long style)

Emerging from a thick, woody rhizome, the
stems are 8" to 32" tall, and branching above. The
leaves are deeply divided into three to five toothed
lobes. The lower leaves are long-petiolate; the upper
leaves sessile. The flowers have five, pale blue-purple
petals with dark rose streaks. The flowers have a faint
sweet fragrance. The pubescent sepals form a
green star behind the petals. The thin style at
the flower's center extends up to an inch long
as the plant matures.

—continues

Cranesbill blooms midsummer and is very abundant on hillsides and meadows, often growing among fleabane *(Erigeron peregrinus),* ferns, and grasses. As the plant matures and drops its petals, each style becomes greatly elongated. Down the sides of the styles run five thin, strong strips, which are attached to a single capsule tucked at the base. When the plant dries, the capsule splits into five one-seeded segments. The strips wind up the style in a spring-loaded curl, each carrying and releasing a hard brown seed. It is interesting to note that all the names given this plant refer to its long, pointed style. The botanical name *Geranium* comes from the Greek *geranos,* meaning crane. The Unangan term *chunusiˆx* is especially descriptive. Medicinal teas were made from both the leaves and the roots. A tea made from the leaves was used as a gargle to soothe sore throats, or when cooled and strained, for washing wounds to help dry infection (Hudson 1992).

The cranesbill's leaves are very similar to those of the poisonous monkshood *(Aconitum* spp.), so be very careful with identification.

RANGE:
Eastern Asia, throughout the Aleutians, southern half of Alaska into British Columbia.

mature plant showing elongated styles

Violet Family / *Violaceae*

Violet, Alaska Violet
Viola langsdorffii Fisch.

Emerging from a thick-ened rhizome, the stems are slender, single-flower-ing, and 2" to 6" tall. The leaves are glabrous and dark green, broadly ovate to cordate, the margins shallowly crenate. The pale to deep violet blossoms have five overlapping pet-als with fine dark veins.

A small plant with blos-soms that offer a delight-ful fragrance, this violet blooms in early spring in damp ground, in meadows, and along stream banks where the snow has melt-ed. In favorable spots they are found in large patches. In late summer when flowering ceases, large green pods form. These later split open into three sharp sections, each hold-ing rows of small black seeds.

RANGE:
Eastern Asia, throughout the Aleutians, southern half of Alaska, Pacific Northwest.

*mature plant
with seed pods*

Evening Primrose Family / *Onagraceae*

The evening primrose family is well represented in the Aleutians by the genus *Epilobium,* the fireweeds and willow herbs. The leaves are simple, sessile, or with short petioles, the margins entire or toothed. The flowers are regular with four sepals and four petals. The flowers are borne on elongate inferior ovaries which are often so slender they resemble the stem below. The ripe linear capsules split open and are filled with tiny seeds each tufted with silky hairs. *Epilobium* is Greek for "upon a pod" and having flowers sitting upon the ovary is the distinguishing feature of all the members of the genus. Species with large and showy flowers *(E. angustifolium* and *E. latifolium)* are the most familiar and easy to recognize. The only species with yellow flowers is *E. luteum.*

The small-flowered species, known as willow herbs, are confusing to identify and extremely variable in form. Described by the best botanists as a taxonomist's nightmare, they have defied even the best efforts at developing a good key for them (Hultén 1960). Found on Unalaska are *E. anagallidifolium, E. leptocarpum, E. behringianum, E. hornemannii,* and *E. sertulatum,* in addition to the species described here.

The flaming leaves of fireweed in the fall.

Evening Primrose Family / Onagraceae

Fireweed
Epilobium angustifolium
L.

(E) *kimliiyax̂, kipriiyax̂,*
from the Russian *kiprey*
(A) *kipriiyas, chikayaasix̂*

Arising from woody rhizomes, the stems are leafy, single, and unbranching, two to six feet tall. The leaves are long and lanceolate, the margins often undulate (wavy), the midvein especially prominent underneath. Flowers are held on a long, showy spike of rose pink to magenta blossoms. Rarely the flowers are white. The flowers have four oval petals and four narrow and pointed reddish sepals.

Working with its partner the bumblebee, the fireweed has adapted a fascinating way of assuring cross-pollination with other plants. The flowers at the bottom of a fireweed spike open and mature first, while the buds at the top are still closed. By the time the topmost flowers are open and bearing their pollen, the ones at the bottom have already shed their pollen and have opened their stigmas, ready to receive pollen from another flower. Here the bumblebee comes in, whose habit it is to start at the bottom of a fireweed spike and climb its way up. Flying off from the top of one spike, dusted with pollen, it lands at the bottom of the next, where the flowers are ready to receive it.

The young shoots can be eaten raw or steamed, and the blossoms make a ruby magenta jelly. The dried leaves make a wonderful tea which has long been used by the Unangan and is often mentioned in their stories. For tea, cut the stems before the flowers bloom and hang them upside down to dry. Once dry, the leaves emit a distinctive, berrylike fragrance.

This common species is the official flower of the Yukon Territory, Canada.

RANGE:
Northern circumpolar.

Dwarf Fireweed, River Beauty
Epilobium latifolium L.

Arising from a woody rootstock, the flowering stems
are 4" to 20" tall, curving upwards from the base and
sometimes branching. The leaves are soft and slightly
succulent, grayish green, elliptic to lanceolate, and
less than 3" long. Flowers are large and showy,
borne at the tips of elongate ovaries, with four
broad, rose-pink petals between the narrow dark
red sepals. The long filaments at the center of the
flower bear a stunning turquoise pollen, like that
of the tall fireweed. Rarely, the flowers are white,
as shown below.

   Dwarf fireweed is a lovely plant of gravel river bars,
dry rocky areas, roadsides, and coastal scree. Although the plants
are shorter and bushier than
E. angustifolium, the flowers are
much larger. The shoots, leaves,
and blossoms of both species can
be used in the same ways.

RANGE:
Northern circumpolar and
throughout Alaska.

White blossoms appear rarely

Yellow Willow Herb
Epilobium luteum Pursh

Ascending from long, branching rhizomes, the stems are leafy, curving, and sometimes branching near the base, 4" to 32" tall. The leaves, held in opposite pairs, are lanceolate, and finely toothed, and up to 3" long. The flowers are pale creamy yellow and often somewhat closed, the petals up to ¾" long and shallowly notched. The flowers are loosely bunched and nodding from the tips of the long narrow ovaries.

The yellow willow herb is the only *Epilobium* in Alaska with yellow flowers. The leafy plants often grow in patches, their showy blossoms nodding along river bars, springs and ditches.

RANGE:
Found through the Pacific Northwest and southern coastal Alaska, it reaches only into the eastern Aleutians.

Trelease Willow Herb
Epilobium treleaseanum
  Levl.
(= *Epilobium x treleasia-*
  num Levl.)

125

Evening Primrose Family / *Onagraceae*

The flowering stems of this plant are up to 8" long. The leaves, held in opposite pairs, are elliptic to lance-olate, finely toothed, and up to 1" long. Flowers vary in color and may be pale yellow, pinkish, or rose purple. The four petals are rounded and shallowly notched, with petals up to ½" long. Sepals are linear to lanceolate, two-thirds the length of the petals. The ovaries are thin, ¾" to 1 ¾" long.

The plant may be a hybrid of *E. luteum* and *E. glandulosum* (Welsh 1974). It favors wet places and mossy seeps, and the showy flowers resemble those of *E. luteum*.

RANGE:
The Alaska Peninsula and eastern Aleutian Islands.

Evening Primrose Family / Onagraceae

Willow Herb, Glandular Willow Herb

Epilobium glandulosum Lehm.
(= *E. ciliatum* Raf. ssp. *glandulosum* (Lehm.) Hoch and Raven

The stems are leafy, mostly simple but sometimes branching near the top, variable in height from 6" to 36" tall. The leaves are up to 4" long and 1 ½" wide, broadly lanceolate, finely toothed, often reddish or red edged. The leaves are mostly sessile; the upper leaves may have short stems. The flowers are small and held above the thin ovaries, mostly bunched at the top of the plant, but also sometimes in the axils of the lower leaves. The flowers are bright pink to lilac purple, often somewhat closed, the petals usually less than ¼" long. The ovaries are reddish and up to 2 ½" long.

This willow herb is common in both grassy fields and damp meadows, and often grows among fireweed *(E. augustifolium),* putchki *(Heracleum lanatum),* and artemisia *(Artemisia* spp.).

RANGE:
Eastern Asia, throughout the Aleutians, Pacific coast of Alaska, Pacific Northwest.

seed capsules opening

Water Milfoil Family / *Haloragaceae*

Mare's Tail
Hippuris vulgaris L.

These aquatic plants grow from an immersed horizontal rhizome. The long, single stems are jointed, bright green, rising 8" to 24" tall above the water's surface. The stems are ringed with whorls of short, narrow, pointed leaves. Minute white flowers appear in the axils of the leaves; the unopened buds are red.

Mare's tail is a beautiful plant of quiet water. It grows in large stands from the muddy bottoms of sloughs, river bends and shallow ponds.

RANGE:
Northern circumpolar and widespread across Alaska.

OTHER SPECIES:
Also found on Unalaska Island is the very small and moss-like mountain mare's tail, *Hippuris montana* Ledeb.

Parsley Family / *Umbelliferae* or *Apiaceae*

**Petruski, Beach Lovage,
Sea Lovage**
Ligusticum scoticum L.
ssp. *hultenii* (Fern.)
Calder & R. Taylor
(= *L. hultenii* Fern.)

qanisan, qanasin, perhaps
from *qanisa:* wait for
eating
pitruuskin, petruski, from
the Russian petrushka

This is a common
and leafy green plant, emerging from a taproot,
with stems 8" to 20" tall. The stems are glabrous
and streaked with red; the young stems are dark
red. The leaves consist of three leaflets; the leaflets are oval shaped and finely toothed;
when young, they are edged in red.
The flowering stem is branching,
bearing tiny, white to pinkish fragrant flowers in lacy, flat-topped
umbels. Later the umbels are
crowded with small oblong
fruits.

—*continues*

Petruski favors dry rocky and sandy areas. It often grows near seashores and cliffs and seems to be salt tolerant. The young leaves and stems are delicious, with a strong, parsley-like, peppery taste. They are excellent eaten raw, used as greens in fish soups, or boiled with trout or salmon. The greens can be dried or frozen for winter use. *Caution:* When petruski is young it can be confused with *Angelica lucida,* a medicinal plant with leaves that cannot be used like petruski. The angelica's leaves are composed of numerous opposite pairs of leaflets along the stem, *ending* in a group of three, whereas the petruski's leaflets are always in a *single* group of three.

RANGE:
Eastern Asia, throughout the Aleutians, coastal Alaska from Bering Strait to British Columbia, Canada.

129

Parsley Family / Umbelliferae or Apiaceae

Young leaves prime for picking

Western Hemlock Parsley
Conioselinum chinense (L.)
BSP.
(= *C. pacificum* (S. Wats.)
J. Coulter & Rose,
C. gmelinii (Cham. &
Schlecht.) Coult. and
Rose

(E) *chikiglux̂. Qalngaaĝim
saaqudaa:* raven's
parsnip
(A) *chikilĝux̂*

Growing from a stout tap-root, the stems are hollow and upright, to 48" tall. The large branching leaves are divided into many finely toothed leaflets. The small white flowers are born on rays in a densely crowded umbel. The fruits are glabrous, oval, to oblong and flattened.

Hemlock parsley often grows in tall grass, and favors meadows, sandy shores, and banks. It is similar to petruski *(Ligusticum scoticum)* and angelica *(Angelica lucida)*, but the leaves are more dissected, like carrot tops, and the plant grows quite tall. By August's end the leaves briefly turn exquisite golden orange and dark red. The Unangan chewed the tender stems to relieve sore throats, and the leaves were dried and used for tea (Hudson 1992). Be careful with this plant, since some look-alikes are deadly poisonous.

RANGE:
Eastern Asia, throughout the Aleutians, coastal Alaska from Bering Strait to the Pacific Northwest.

Seacoast Angelica, St. Paul Putchki, Strong Putchki
Angelica lucida L.
(= *Coelopleurum gmelinii*)

(E) *saaqudiigamax̂, saaqdigimagax̂, suqudmix̂*
(A) *saaqudax̂*
(E) *sxilax̂, simx̂ux̂*, also possibly other parsley family members

Seacoast angelica is a coarse, stout, leafy plant emerging from a thick
and tuberous root. The stems are hollow, 20" to 48" tall, and often red-
dish-streaked. The compound leaves emerge from a sheathlike base, and
the numerous leaflets are held in opposite pairs along the petiole, ending
in a group of three leaflets. The leaflets are glabrous and fairly thick, ovate
and unevenly serrate. The tiny, fragrant, greenish-white flowers are held in
a flat-topped, many-rayed umbel. As the plant matures the umbel becomes
densely clustered with slightly flattened oval fruits.

Seacoast angelica sends its leaves up very early in the spring, before
many other plants are conspicuous. It looks very much like petruski, or
beach lovage *(Ligusticum scoticum)*, and is easily mistaken for it when the
plant is young. The leaves of *Ligusticum* always consist of a single group
of three leaflets with no additional pairs of leaflets. Mature angelica plants
are taller and much thicker-stemmed than petruski, with larger umbels.

—continues

Seacoast angelica is regarded more as a medicinal plant than an edible one, and in fact some references claim parts of the plant to be poisonous. The stems, carefully peeled and eaten like the putchki, *Heracleum lanatum,* are occasionally used by the Unangan people. Seacoast angelica was used medicinally by the Unangan. The leaves were used as a poultice, and the roots eased pain, aching muscles and cramps. The root was sliced in half, heated, and placed over the area in pain. These heated roots were said to ease pain even deep within the body (Banks 1962). The root was never placed directly on the skin, but soft grass or cloth was used in between (N. Galaktianoff, Sr., pers. com.). Eric Hultén (1968), noted that in Siberia, angelica root was carried as an amulet to ward off polar bears, and the fumes of the roasted root were inhaled as a remedy for seasickness.

RANGE:
Eastern Asia, widespread across Alaska, Pacific Northwest.

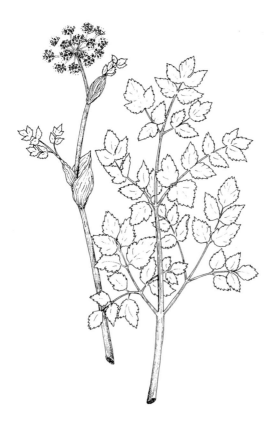

132

Parsley Family / *Umbelliferae* or *Apiaceae*

Putchki (from the Russian), Cow Parsnip, Wild Celery
Heracleum lanatum Michx.

(E) *saaqudax̂*
(A) *taaĝangix̂*

This is a huge, spreading plant with tall, jointed stalks, and a stout, woody taproot. The whole plant often stands head high. The stems are hollow and thick. Leaves are large, flat, and crinkled, thrice divided and coarsely toothed. The leaves emerge from large woolly sheaths. The small white flowers are borne in a many-rayed umbel, forming large, flat heads. When the plant dries, the stalks turn silvery black and brittle; the flower tops turn black and seedy, looking burned.

The putchki is a favorite plant of sparrows, finches, and wrens, and in the spring it is not uncommon to see a nest-bound eagle winging overhead with a putchki stalk dangling from her talons. In the treeless Aleutians they are used as nesting material. Putchki favors grassy hillsides and meadows, often growing near beaches and old village sites, among monkshood (*Aconitum* spp.), fireweed (*Epilobium* spp.), and buttercups (*Ranunculus* spp.).

—continues

When the plants are young, part of the stem is edible when peeled. The middle section of the stalk, between the branches of the upper and lower leaves, is the best part. Cut the plant near the base of the stem. Grasp and pull out the upper sheath to expose the tender inner stalk. Carefully peeled, it is crunchy, sweet, and celerylike. It is good munched raw, chopped into salads and soups, pickled or dipped in seal oil. Avoid older plants and those with stems streaked with red; their juice can cause blistering burns on hands and arms and around the mouth. Wild rhubarb (*Rumex fenestratus*) can be used to soothe these burns by applying the juice from the stems or leaves (N. Galaktianoff, Sr., pers. comm.). The Unangan used the putchki's leaves to poultice sore muscles and brewed them as a tea for colds (Hudson 1992). The rubbed leaves were also used to remove the human scent from hands and bait when halibut fishing (B. Golodoff pers. comm.).

RANGE:
Eastern Asia, throughout the Aleutians, widespread across Alaska, Canada, and the United States.

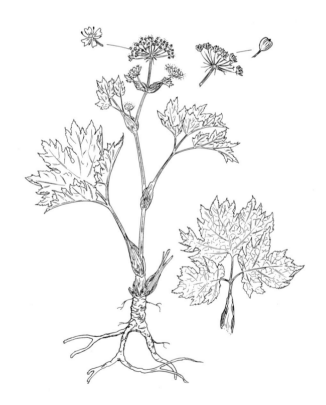

Dogwood Family / *Cornaceae*

Dwarf Dogwood, Bunchberry, Lapland or Swedish Dwarf Cornel
Cornus suecica L.

This is a lovely, low-growing, white-flowered plant. Emerging from rhizomes, the flowering stems are upright, 4" to 12" tall. The oval, pointed leaves, with distinct parallel veins, are held in whorls around the stem. What appears to be four broad white petals are actually petaloid bracts. They often have what looks like a rosy stain. The bracts surround a dense cluster of tiny flowers which later develop into shiny red berries. The berries are pulpy and rather inedible, but not poisonous.

Dwarf dogwood is common in the crowberry heath and dry meadows and often covers large areas. In the fall the leaves turn scarlet and ruddy purple.

—*continues*

Dogwood Family / *Cornaceae*

RANGE:
Circumboreal and found throughout the Aleutians.

A hybrid between *Cornus suecica* and a close relative which is very rare in the eastern Aleutians, Canadian dwarf cornel *(Cornus canadensis)*, is also found on Unalaska, *Cornus canadensis* L. x *suecica* L. (= *C. unalaschensis* Ledeb.). This plant usually has only two leaf whorls along the stem, with leaves in the upper whorl being much larger than those below. The tiny flowers on the hybrid may be yellowish green, or at least lighter than the purplish black flowers seen on *C. suecica*. Considerable variation exists among these three dwarf dogwoods and the technical descriptions found in Hultén (1960, 1968) may be needed to identify them.

fall foliage

Wintergreen Family / *Pyrolaceae*

Pyrola, Wintergreen
Pyrola asarifolia Michx.

137

The single flowering stems are glabrous and leafless (except for a few small bracts), pale green, and 6" to 12" tall. They rise well above the few basal leaves which are petiolate, shiny and leathery; the blades are rounded and some-what variable in shape. The leaf blades are up to about 2" in diameter. The top few inches of the flowering stem bear numerous small blossoms which are held on very short stems. The closed buds resemble rose red balls which open into nodding, dark pink bells. Only the topmost flowers are held upright. The lower flowers open first, and the long, slender, and curving style extends outside the blossom.

This pyrola is a delicate bloom of meadows, fields, and hillsides, often growing among ferns, bistort *(Polygonum viviparum),* and fleabane *(Erigeron peregrinus).* In the fall the flowering stems turn dry and brittle, but the leaves stay green all through the winter snows. These wintergreen leaves begin photosynthesis early in the spring, and only after the plant forms new leaves do the old ones finally wither.

RANGE:
Widespread across Russia, Japan, Alaska, and North America; lacking in the central Aleutians.

**Pyrola, Lesser
Wintergreen**
Pyrola minor L.

The single flowering stems
are glabrous and leafless,
often reddish, 2" to 8" tall.
The basal leaves are dime
sized, glabrous and short
petiolate, and held close to
the ground. The top inch
or two of the stem bears
the numerous small flow-
ers, which are held on very
short stems.

The flowers are light
pink, nodding, and bell
shaped and never fully
open. Even the topmost
flowers all point
downward. The flower's style is straight and does not extend outside the flower.

Lesser wintergreen is a plant of meadows and damp tundra.
With its delicate nodding pink bells, it is similar to the taller
P. asariflora but its leaves are much smaller and it is not nearly as
common here.

RANGE:
Northern circumpolar, throughout the Aleutians.

OTHER SPECIES:
Single-sided
pyrola, or side-
bells wintergreen,
Pyrola secunda L.
(=*Orthilia secunda*
(L.) House) is very
scarce but found at upper
elevations among the heath. The
small white flowers are held along
one side of the stem.

*Left: Single-sided pyrola, or sidebells
wintergreen, Pyrola secunda L. (=
Orthilia secunda (L.) House)*

Crowberry Family / *Empetraceae*

Mossberry, Blackberry, Crowberry
Empetrum nigrum L.

(E) *qaayum qaxchikluu:* black berry, from *qaayux̂:* berry, and
   qaxchiklux̂: black. *kidngax̂, kidngam qaayuu:* mossberry
(A) *kingdam aangsuu,* from *kingdax̂:* mossberry bush or patch,
   and *aangsux̂:* berry, especially a mossberry
(Attu) *kigyax̂, askugit*

A low-growing evergreen, heath-like shrub, mossberry has long, slender
mat-forming branches. The leaves are dark green, short, narrow, and
needlelike, and whorled around the branches. The purple flowers, which
bloom in early May, are very tiny and inconspicuous, held in the axils of
the upper leaves. The berries are small, black, and hard-skinned. Two
subspecies have been described, which overlap in our area according to
Hultén (1968). The subspecies *nigrum* has imperfect flowers; the male
and female flowers are on separate plants, explaining why their berries are
found in patches. The subspecies *hermaphroditum* bears perfect flowers
and slightly larger seeds and fruits.

—continues

This plant forms the deep, springy hillcover of crowberry heath so soft to flop down in when hiking and berrying. *Empetrum* means "upon rock," and the dense shrub forms a mantle over these volcanic islands, holding the soil against wind and erosion. The plant was once used as fuel by Unangan and it makes good tinder. It was also used as mattress material. Mossberries grow in patches and are often so thick they can be combed into a bucket with one's fingers or a berry-picker. The berries are good eaten fresh, cooked into jams and jellies and also make excellent pies, alone or mixed with blueberries. Before the time of refrigeration, mossberries were stored in barrels of water; in winter the ice was broken and the berries dipped out.

Aleutian heather, *Phyllodoce aleutica*, looks very similar to the mossberry plant, but its leaves are slightly larger. Aleutian heather bears clusters of small pale yellow, urn-shaped flowers, and does not produce berries.

RANGE:
Circumpolar; widespread in the Aleutians.

Crowberry Family / *Empetraceae*

Heath Family / *Ericaceae*

Heaths are low-growing shrubs with simple leaves. In many species the leaves are stiff, leathery, and evergreen. The flowers are composed of four or five fused sepals and four or five petals which are also partly united or fused together. The family includes the familiar two species of blueberries *(Vaccinium ovalifolium, V. uliginosum)*, the lingonberry *(Vaccinium vitis-idea)*, alpine bearberry *(Arctostaphylos alpina)*, and kinnikinnick *(Arctostaphylos uva-ursi)*, and the Aleutian heathers *(Phyllodoce aleutica)* and moss heather *(Cassiope lycopodioides)*, all of which are recognized by their small urn-shaped blossoms. The tiny alpine azalea *(Loiseleuria procumbens)*, and the showy Kamchatka rhododendron *(Rhododendron camtschaticum)* have more open flowers; their petals are fused only at the base. The bog cranberry's *(Oxycoccus microcarpus)* flower is unique and much like a shooting star; its petals are bent backwards or reflexed.

A large and diverse family of worldwide distribution, the heaths are important in the north and make up a large proportion of the plant cover. Members of the family often grow together in heath communities, forming a thickly woven mantle over vast regions. Heaths thrive in cold, moist, and acidic soils that are sometimes difficult for other plants. They are able to do this through a special symbiotic relationship between their roots and certain fungi in the soil. The fungus forms a fine extensive web of tubular filaments that penetrate and become part of the plants' roots, enhancing their uptake of nutrients. Heaths are often the first plants to cover bare or exposed ground, providing protection from erosion and shelter for other species to take hold. A common sight is trailing branches of kinnikinnick reaching across open frost-heaved soil or spilling over cutbanks and slides.

In the Aleutians, once away from the beach, either atop the bluffs or just beyond the tall grass near sea level, the heath family is everywhere. At lower elevations tall growth of grasses and other herbaceous plants prevails through the undercover, but in the foothills and higher up as the grass thins out, the heath spreads a dark green cloak. Examining a mere square foot will reveal an incredible number of plants, and many are in the heath family. A sample patch is likely underwoven with Aleutian heather and threaded through with lingonberry and kinnikinnick. On steep slopes Kamchatka rhododendrons thrive. Up high and on drier ground, one may find leathery bearberry leaves and delicate moss heather. All this provides a hold for members of other families: the trailing stems of twinflower *(Linnaea borealis)* and the long yellow rhizomes of goldthread *(Coptis trifolia)*. Tufts of sphagnum moss and sprawling devil's belt poke through,

—*continues*

and nestled in among them, pyrola (*Pyrola* spp.) and dwarf dogwood (*Cornus* spp.). In the summer myriad wildflowers reach up through the cover, but it's during the winter, when all else is gone and only the evergreen growth remains that the prevalence of the heath family may best be realized.

Alpine Azalea
Loiseleuria procumbens (L.) Desv.

This is a very low-growing dwarf shrub with trailing branches that form dense mats. The tiny pink flowers have five petals and five stamens. The stiff and leathery evergreen leaves are oblong and even smaller than the flowers, usually less than ¼" long.

Alpine azalea forms a dense ground cover over rocky areas, roadsides and stony tundra. A small sprig laid in a saucer of water looks like an exquisite flowering bonsai.

RANGE:
Northern circumpolar and widespread in Alaska.

Kamchatka Rhododendron
Rhododendron camtschaticum Pall.

This is a woody low-growing shrub with branches 2" to 12" tall. The branches are covered with
grayish brown bark and bear dark green, oblong to
obovate leaves. Leaves are red edged with fine hairs
along the margins. Flowers are a deep rose purple;
the five bright petals encircle ten long curving filaments, and the even longer style. The sepals are reddish and covered with fine hairs. In the fall the leaves
turn ruddy orange and the flowering stems dry stiff. The
blossoms drop but the five sepals remain like a star around
the dry oblong seed capsule. The long style persists, curling
out from the tip of the capsule.

Kamchatka rhododendron is a lovely and showy flower that
covers hillsides and steep slopes. It is a beautiful plant for drying
and pressing; the glowing magenta petals dry a dark purple.

RANGE:
From Japan and Kamchatka, throughout the Aleutian Islands; scattered
populations along the Pacific coast of Alaska.

Aleutian Heather
Phyllodoce aleutica (Spreng.) Heller

This is a common, low-growing evergreen shrub that forms a dense ground cover, with branches usually 2" to 7" tall. The tiny leaves are needlelike, short, narrow and stiff, and densely whorled around the stems. The pale yellow urn-shaped blossoms are borne in clusters from the tips of the branches. The fruit is a small dry capsule.

Aleutian heather covers vast areas of the island, blanketing hillsides and slopes. As are many members of the heath family, it is evergreen, and the leaves are tolerant of freezing. As an evergreen, its energy demands are lower than those of deciduous plants. The older leaves store food, and extensive new leaf growth is not needed every year.

RANGE:
Japan, Kamchatka, throughout the Aleutian Islands, along the Pacific coast of Alaska.

Club-Moss Mountain Heather
Cassiope lycopodioides
(Pall.) D. Don

This heather is a low-growing plant with delicate, trailing mosslike branches. The tiny oval leaves are tightly pressed against the branches and overlap like scales in four rows, giving the thin branches a squared look. The branches, including the leaves, are less than ⅛" wide. The delicate flowers hang singly from the tips of red, threadlike pedicels, which emerge upright near the tips of the branches. The flowers are small, white, bell-shaped, and a mere ¼" long.

This plant grows rather sparsely at upper elevations, in the dry tundra of slopes and knolls, often among lingonberry *(Vaccinium vitis-idea)* and alpine bearberry *(Arctostaphylos alpina).*

RANGE:
Japan, Kamchatka, throughout the Aleutians, Pacific coast of Alaska.

OTHER SPECIES:
Cassiope stelleriana (Pall.) DC.

Kinnikinnick, Mealberry, Bearberry
Arctostaphylos uva-ursi (L.) Spreng.

(E) *hulâx̂, ulâx̂, ulâĝin*

Kinnikinnick is an abundant plant forming a ground cover with trailing stems. The long, woody, flexible branches are covered with leathery, teardrop-shaped green leaves. Blooming early, it bears clusters of small, pale pink, urn-shaped flowers, later forming bright red berries. The berries have applelike, pithy white centers. They are edible but not especially tasty.

Kinnikinnick favors hillsides and slopes, often trailing over cutbanks and bluff tops. It is an evergreen plant, and both leaves and berries appear unscathed during intermittent snows and thaws. Even under feet of snow, digging reveals the supple green foliage and plump red berries.

The long branches can be twined into a winter wreath. The berries are said to taste best late in the year, after it has snowed and melted again (N. Galaktianoff, Sr., pers. com.).

RANGE:
Circumboreal and widespread in Alaska, lacking in the central and western Aleutians.

Alpine Bearberry
Arctostaphylos alpina (L.) Spreng.
(=*Arctous alpina* (L.) Niedenzu)

(E) *qalngaag̑im qaayuu:* raven's berry

A low-growing woody shrub with stiff branches, alpine bearberry grows 1" to 4" tall. The ovate leaves are finely toothed, leathery, reticulate, and rough textured. The small flowers are pale yellow and urn shaped. The fruit is a blue-black berry.

Alpine bearberry is not an abundant or especially tasty berry, although it is edible. It grows in dry heath-covered tundra and on rocky knolls, often tucked among reindeer lichen. The leaves are very similar to those of the net leaf willow *(Salix reticulata),* and the two plants favor the same habitat. But while the alpine bearberry's leaf tapers to its base, the net leaf willow's is rounded where it meets the stem. In fall, the alpine bearberry's brilliant orange red foliage is striking among the dark rocky outcroppings.

RANGE:
Northern circumpolar and widespread in Alaska, lacking in central and western Aleutians.

148

*Above and right: berries
and striking foliage of*
Arctostaphylos alpina

*Below: colorful Heath family
members: highbush blueberry
at left, lowbush blueberry
at right, and Kamchatka
rhododendron's bright orange
leaves at upper center.*

Lingonberry, Mountain Cranberry
Vaccinium vitis-idaea L.

(E) *kiikax̂*
(A) *tuyangis*
(Russian) *brusnika*, probably also names for the cranberry
(*Oxycoccus microcarpus*)

A delicate evergreen plant with thin, reddish-brown stems, lingonberry seldom grows more than a few inches tall. The leaves are very small, usually about ¼" long. They are ovate, dark green, stiff, and leathery, with a deep crease down the middle. The pale pink urn-shaped flowers are borne in clusters at the tips of the stems. Later they form small red berries about ¼" long.

Lingonberries spread in low patches over the dry tundra of hillsides and knolls, often growing among other members of the heath family. Lingonberry is superficially similar to kinnikinnick, but is usually smaller and has shiny leaves and a juicy berry. The tart berries turn a darker translucent red and become juicy late in the season. They are best picked in October and even November.

RANGE:
Northern circumpolar and widespread in Alaska.

Blueberry, Highbush or Early Blueberry
Vaccinium ovalifolium Smith

(E) *unignax̂, unignan, unisan*

Blueberry bushes tend to grow in patches. They are usually waist to shoulder high, with sturdy branches, and thin angled branchlets. Older bushes become dense and woody and their branches look bleached. The leaves are ovate and glabrous, bright green and thin in the spring, turning flaming orange and yellow in the fall. The pale pink urn-shaped flowers bloom very early in spring, appearing when the shrub just begins to leaf out. From late August to early November the bushes bear an abundance of juicy, round blue berries.

—*continues*

Blueberry shrubs are wonderfully abundant in Unalaska's hills and ravines. In good locations like sunny creek beds and damp, well-drained slopes, the branches will bend with the weight of the fruit, and the bushes look blue, even from a distance. Locally picked by the gallon for jams, jellies, pies, and freezing, the berries are tart and juicy, sweetening some after fall frosts begin. They are easier to pick in the fall when most of the leaves have fallen. Good ways to separate the leaves from the berries are to pour them between buckets and let the wind sift the leaves out, or fill the bucket with water and skim off the floating leaves.

Before winter sets in, blueberry bushes send out new red-tipped growth with buds, ready for the first hint of spring. It flowers early and rapidly develops fruit during our short, cool summers. The buds on these new red sprigs will bloom in a jar of water, even in February, when you cannot wait for spring any longer. The tender little buds are also a favorite food of ptarmigan.

RANGE:
Pacific Northwest, southern (mostly coastal) Alaska to eastern Aleutians.

151

Heath Family / *Ericaceae*

152

Alpine Blueberry, Bog or Lowbush Blueberry
Vaccinium uliginosum L.

(E) *ugiidĝin, ux̂iidngin, ux̂iidgin*
(A) *muĝuzaalĝis*

Alpine blueberry is a low-growing, strongly branched, dwarf shrub, 4" to 24" tall. The leaves are broadly elliptic to rounded, usually less than ½" long. The small urn-shaped blossoms are rosy pink. The berries are dusty blue, ovate, and less than ½" long.

Compared with the highbush blueberry (*V. ovalifolium*), the leaves are much smaller and rounder. Also, the blossoms are a deeper pink, and the dusty-blue berries are smaller, ovate, and have a much milder taste. While not nearly so abundant as *V. ovalifolium*, alpine blueberries can be found in prolific little patches. In late fall the leaves turn crimson orange.

RANGE:
Northern circumpolar, widespread across Alaska into eastern Aleutians.

Cranberry, Bog Cranberry, Shooting Star
Oxycoccus microcarpus Turcz.

(E) *kiikax̂*
(A) *tuyangis*
(Russian) *brusnika*. These are probably also names for the lingonberry
  (*Vaccinium vitis-idaea*)

This is a delicate plant whose slender creeping stems root in wet ground.
The leathery leaves are lance shaped and very tiny, less than ¼" long. The
reddish, threadlike flowering stems hold tiny dark pink blossoms with four
reflexed petals. The plant later bears tiny tart cranberries, though not in
abundance here.

   Bog cranberry grows among mosses and sundews (*Drosera rotundifolia*)
in wet meadows and bogs. It needs wetter habitat than the lingonberry (*Vaccinium vitis-idea*), whose fruit is similar.

RANGE:
Northern circumpolar, widespread across Alaska; lacking in
the central Aleutians.

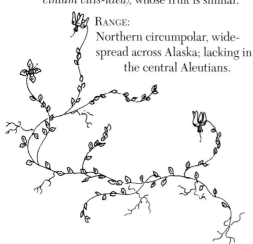

Primrose Family / *Primulaceae*

Chukchi Primrose
Primula tschuktschorum
Kjellm. var. *arctica*
(Koidz.) Fern.
(= *P. eximia* E. Greene)

Emerging from slender fibrous roots, the leaves form a basal rosette. The leaves are oblong to bluntly lanceolate, to 3" long or more, fleshy and with a prominent mid-vein underneath. The margins are nearly entire or with small, shallowly rounded teeth (crenulate), and the leaf edges often curl backwards. The flowering stem is leafless, stout, dark purple, and up to 10" tall. The tip of the stem bears an umbel of few to several purple flowers. Each flower has five rounded unnotched lobes, and a white eye. The corolla tube is much longer than the calyx, which is dark purple to almost black, and two-thirds cleft. The upper stem, pedicels, and calyx are sometimes coated with a white flour-like dust. As the plant matures and the blossoms drop, elongated seed capsules form and are held in an erect cluster at the tip of the stem. The capsules extend twice the length of the calyx or more.

The Chukchi primrose is Alaska's largest and perhaps most exquisite primrose. The species is highly variable. Here on Unalaska Island it is very scarce and only found in scattered locations. It blooms in early June in the wet meadows and seeps of upper elevations. Flowers this rare should not be picked; the joy is in finding them and seeing them grow.

The wedge-leaved primrose (*P. cuneifolia*) is a similar but much more common species, easily distinguished by the five deeply notched lobes and yellow eye of its flowers.

RANGE:
Scattered throughout the Aleutians and along both sides of the Bering Sea, also found in the interior of Alaska to the edge of the Yukon.

Primrose, Wedge-leaved Primrose
Primula cuneifolia Ledeb.

Emerging from slender fibrous roots, the leaves form a basal rosette. The leaves are glabrous, cuneate (wedge-shaped), and toothed toward the tip, tapering to a short petiole. The leaves are usually less than 2" long, including their stem. The flowering stem is leafless, 2" to 4" tall, bearing at its tip one to several violet-pink flowers.

The corolla tube is slightly longer than the calyx; the five lobes are each deeply notched, and the flower has a yellow eye.

Although sparse and particular about its habitat, the wedge-leaved primrose can be found from sea level up to the windswept ridges. This small jewel of a flower prefers damp, often rocky, locations where the vegetation is low.

RANGE:
Eastern Asia, western Alaska, and throughout the Aleutian Islands; scattered populations along the Pacific coast of Alaska.

OTHER SPECIES:
Also found, but very scarce, is the inconspicuous Greenland Primrose, *Primula egaliksensis* Wormsk.

Starflower, Arctic Starflower
Trientalis europaea L. ssp. *arctica* (Fisch.) Hult.

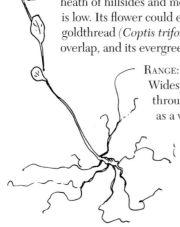

Emerging from slender rhizomes, the stems are upright, often less than 4" tall. Leaves are reddish green, broadly elliptic, and bunched or whorled at midstem. Long slender pedicels ascend above the leaves, each bearing a single, white flower that is delicate and lovely. The small flower usually has seven overlapping, pointed corolla lobes, a tiny yellow center, and pink anthers held on long filaments.

Starflower grows among the moss and crowberry heath of hillsides and meadows where the ground cover is low. Its flower could easily be mistaken for that of the goldthread (*Coptis trifolia*), but goldthread petals do not overlap, and its evergreen leaves are sharply toothed.

RANGE:
Widespread across Alaska and found throughout the Aleutians, the species as a whole is circumboreal.

156

Primrose Family / *Primulaceae*

Gentian Family / *Gentianaceae*

Northern Gentian
Gentiana amarella L.
(= *Gentianella amarella*
  (L.) Boerner, *Gentiana*
  acuta Michx.)

Arising from a pale, slender taproot, the stem is upright, squared with beveled edges, and 6" to 12" tall. The basal leaves are obovate to spatulate. The stem leaves are narrowly lanceolate, up to 1½" long, clasping, and somewhat cordate at the base, and held in upward-pointing, opposite pairs. The flowers are mostly crowded at the top, but are also held on short stems which emerge from the axils of the stem leaves, or sometimes from the base of the plant. The flowers are usually pale violet to lilac, but are occasionally cream colored. Close examination reveals their typical gentian shape. The flowers have four to five short, pointed corolla lobes encircling a narrow tube. The lobes are shorter than the tube itself, and the flowers are fringed on the inside with soft hairs. The green sepals are narrow and slightly shorter than the tube.

The northern gentian is fairly common and favors dry areas from sea level up, often growing in poor soil. The Aleutian gentian, similar but quite rare here, has shorter stems and lacks the fringe of hairs inside its flowers.

RANGE:
Northern circumpolar; Asia, the Aleutians, across southern Alaska into North America.

Aleutian Gentian
Gentiana aleutica Cham. & Schlecht.
(= *Gentianella propinqua* (Richardson) J.M. Gillett. ssp. *aleutica* (Cham. & Schlecht.) J.M. Gillett.)

Arising from a pale, slender taproot, the stem is purplish, twisted, wing-angled or beveled, and 1 ½" to 4" tall. The basal leaves are obovate to spatulate. The stem leaves are more broadly lanceolate to elliptic, up to ¾" long and nearly half as wide. They clasp the stem in upward-pointing, opposite pairs. The flowers are held mostly at the top, but also from shorter, slender stems which emerge from the axils of the stem leaves or from the base of the plant. The flowers are usually blue to violet; dried specimens fade to almost yellow. The flowers are funnel shaped, with four long, pointed corolla lobes that taper down into a tube, these lobes being nearly as long as the tube itself. The flowers are not fringed with hair inside like those of the northern gentian. Two of the four green sepals are broader than the others, and longer than the flower's tube.

Aleutian gentian is a rare flower found in the dry tundra vegetation of upper elevations. It tends to grow higher up than does the northern gentian (*G. amarella* L.).

RANGE:
Throughout the Aleutians.

Waterleaf Family / *Hydrophyllaceae*

Mist Maiden
Romanzoffia unalaschcensis
Cham.

The underground part of the stem is covered with persistent, woody layers. The short-petiolate leaves are crowded at the base of the plant and held below the longer flowering stems. The leaves are round to cordate, scalloped with six to eight rounded teeth, green but often with red edges, and with glandular hairs beneath.

The flowering stems are reddish, pubescent, 3" to 8" tall, and branching near the top to hold the flowers. The numerous nodding bell-shaped flowers are white, with five lobes and yellow centers. The pubescent sepals are reddish green and two-thirds the length of the petals.

Mist maiden grows from sea level up, in moist rocky areas and slopes. It is often mistaken for a saxifrage, and the plants favor the same sort of habitat. But the mist maiden's fruit is a single round capsule, whereas most saxifrage have a double-beaked fruit.

RANGE:
Eastern Aleutians to Kodiak Island.

Borage Family / *Boraginaceae*

Oysterleaf, Sea Lungwort
Mertensia maritima (L.) S. F. Gray

A low-growing, spreading plant, with horizontal stems, 8" to 24" long, oysterleaf forms a loose mat. The grayish-blue green leaves are fleshy, ovate to broadly oval shaped, and pointed. Flowers are borne in clusters extending from the axils of the terminal leaves. The tiny buds are pink, but open into blue funnel-shaped flowers. Rarely, the flowers may be white. Later the plant forms small rounded clusters of little dry fruits (nutlets).

Oysterleaf is a coastal plant similar in habit and appearance to the beach green (*Honckenya peploides*) but not nearly as common. It usually prefers cobble or gravel beaches rather than sand. The plant can be found in scattered locations, growing along the shore near the driftwood line, often among beach greens (*Honckenya peploides*), bedstraw (*Galium aparine*), and seabeach senecio (*Senecio pseudo-arnica*). The succulent leaves are mild and good tasting and can be eaten raw or steamed.

RANGE:
Northern circumpolar, along the entire coast of Alaska and throughout the Aleutians to eastern Asia.

Mint Family / *Labiatae* or *Lamiaceae*

Self-heal, Heal-all, Woundwort
Prunella vulgaris L.

Plants emerge from fibrous taproots, and often root from short rhizomes. The stems are usually single, occasionally branching, pubescent, and are 3" to 12" tall. The soft leaves are held in opposite pairs. They are oblong to lanceolate, usually less than 4" long; the margins have a few shallow teeth. The flowers are borne in a dense spike. The layers of dark purple, pubescent bracts form an unusual conelike top, 1" to 3" long. Extending from the bracts is a sparse cluster of bright purple, tubelike flowers. Rarely, plants will bear pink flowers.

Self-heal is a short and curious-looking plant that tends to grow in patches along riverbanks and in low meadows and fields. Unlike many plants in the mint family, the leaves are not fragrant. The flowers keep well when picked and hung upside down to dry.

Self-heal has medicinal uses reported from other areas, including as a tea beneficial for internal disorders and as a wash for external wounds.

RANGE:
Alaska populations of this plant are widely scattered in the Aleutians, the Interior, and Southeastern.

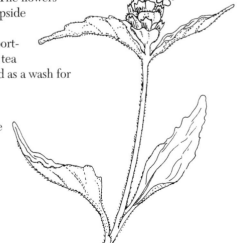

Figwort Family / *Scrophulariaceae*

The figwort family is an interesting one, well represented in the Aleutians. The plants often bear splendid and brightly colored flowers. The leaves and types of flower arrangements vary within the family. The flowers are perfect and composed of four to five united petals that usually form an irregular flower. This means that the flower parts are not similar in size or arrangement, but are bilaterally symmetrical; a line drawn down the middle of the flower would show the two halves to be alike. Only the genus *Veronica*, or speedwells, have nearly radially symmetrical flowers. Most of our figwort flowers form a tube that is distinctly two-lipped. There are usually four stamens and the fruit is a two-valved capsule, often containing many seeds.

Among our favorites are the yellow monkey flower *(Mimulus guttatus)* and coastal paintbrush *(Castilleja unalaschcensis)*, the curious yellow rattle *(Rhinanthus minor)*, the lovely blue speedwells *(Veronica* spp.), the fragrant lagotis *(Lagotis glauca)*, the tiny eyebright *(Euphrasia mollis)*, and the exquisite louseworts *(Pedicularis* spp.).

Louseworts are often given the name "bumblebee flower" because the blossom's tubular shape is adapted for pollination by bees. The flower tips forward as the bee crawls in, the stigma bends and collects pollen from the bee, and the snug fit inside dusts the bee with new pollen that is carried out.

Two figwort family members: lavender chamisso lousewort in the foreground and yellow coastal paintbrush at center.

Yellow Monkey Flower
Mimulus guttatus DC.

kulukuunchikas, from the
   Russian
kolokolchik: small bell

Emerging from rhi-
zomes, the stems are leafy,
branching near the top, to
two feet tall or more. The
upper leaves are rounded
and irregularly toothed,
held in opposite pairs, and
attached directly to the
stem.

The flowers are large and bright yellow
with red freckles inside. The upper lip is two
lobed, the lower lip three lobed and longer.
The green sepals sit like a cap behind the
tubular corolla.

Growing in bright patches, often
near the coast, the monkey flower
is a cheery roadside companion.
Always near water, it favors stream
sides and ditches, gravel bars, and
springs.

RANGE:
Western North America, the southern
half of Alaska, throughout the Aleutians.

Brooklime
Veronica americana Schwein.

The stems root at the nodes or ascend from rhizomes. The stems are weak and curving, glabrous and succulent, 8" to 24" tall. The leaves are lanceolate and gently serrated and up to 3" long. They are opposite and short petioled, glabrous, and often reddish green. Long thin stems ascend from the axils of the leaves, bearing numerous tiny, pale blue flowers. The flowers have four petals and are less than ¼" across.

Brooklime is recognized by its loose and bending stems and the delicate sprinkling of tiny blue flowers. It grows along springs, streams, and roadsides.

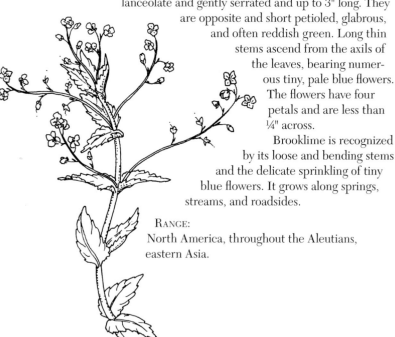

RANGE:
North America, throughout the Aleutians, eastern Asia.

Alpine Speedwell
Veronica wormskjoldii
Roemer & Schultes

The single flowering stem is 4" to 12" tall, often reddish and pubescent, especially near the top. The leaves, also pubescent, are oblong to lanceolate. They are two to three times longer than broad, and up to 1 ½" long and ½" wide. The margins are slightly serrate to entire. They are attached directly to the stem and held in opposite pairs. The pairs of leaves stop 1" to 2" below the flower cluster. Very small and narrow leafy bracts appear among the flowers. The flowers are held in a close group on very short pedicels, almost in a spike. The flowers are violet to dark blue purple, and the four petals are usually of equal size.

The alpine speedwell is uncommon here, found in scattered meadows, damp places, and stream banks. Although typical specimens are easily distinguished from the Steller speedwell *(V. stelleri),* intermediates and possible hybrids exist between the two. The similarities are such that early authors considered them both as variations under the name *Veronica alpina* (Hultén 1960, 1968). Of the plants found on Unalaska Island, the alpine speedwell is the taller of the two. Its leaves are lanceolate and only slightly serrate. *V. stelleri* leaves are ovate, barely twice as long as they are broad, and the margins are noticeably serrate, especially on the upper leaves. Also, the *V. stelleri* flower cluster is typically more open; the flowers are held on pedicels which are ½" long or more.

RANGE:
Southern half of Alaska, eastern and central Aleutians.

Speedwell, Low or Thyme-Leaved Speedwell
Veronica serpyllifolia L.
   ssp. *humifusa* (Dickson)
   Syme
(= *V. tenella* All., *V. humifu-sa* Dickson)

Stems of this speedwell root at the nodes or ascend from rhizomes. Flowering stems are upright, 2" to 12" tall, while the lower leafy stems are often bending. The stems are ribbed and barely pubescent. The lower leaves are up to an inch long, oval, rounded on the ends, the margins gently serrated to entire. The leafy bracts on the flowering stems are small and narrow. The flowers are held on short thin stems branching from the axils of these bracts. The flowers are tiny and light blue. The four petals are tinged with white and have dark veins, and the petals are often of unequal size.

Rather uncommon, this speedwell prefers damp places and stream banks.

It is similar to the common brooklime (*V. americana*) but the flowering stems are more upright, and the leaves are smaller and rounded.

RANGE:
Northern circumpolar, throughout the Aleutians.

Speedwell, Steller Speedwell
Veronica stelleri Pall.

The single, reddish stems are usually less than 6" tall. The leaves are ovate, serrated, and up to 1 ½" long and ¾" broad. Typically, the leaves are barely twice as long as they are broad. They are held in opposite pairs ascending crosswise up the stem. The flowers are held in a cluster just above the leaves, on thin pedicels up to ½" long. The flowers are pale blue to violet, and up to nearly ½" across. The four rounded corolla lobes are often of unequal size, and some of them are so deeply notched as to appear as separate petals.

Steller speedwell's delightful blue flowers are comparatively large for the plant's small size. The other *Veronica* species in our area have similar but much smaller flowers, except the Aleutian speedwell (*V. grandiflora*), which is found only in the central and western Aleutians.

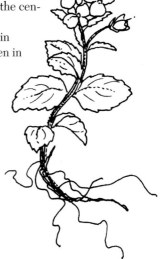

The Steller speedwell is often found blooming in open habitats in both meadows and stony soil, often in dry stream beds and at upper elevations.

Possible hybrids, however, exist between the Steller and alpine speedwells, so it can be hard to tell them apart. See the discussion under alpine speedwell.

RANGE:
Eastern Asia, throughout the Aleutians, along the Pacific Coast of Alaska.

Lagotis, Weasel Snout
Lagotis glauca Gaertn.

The flowering stems are glabrous and thick, often lying down but curving upwards at the tip, up to 12" long. The basal leaves are glabrous, large and oblong, with rounded teeth and wavy margins. The stem leaves are smaller, oval shaped, and clasping. The flowers are held in a cylindrical spike. The very fragrant, tubelike blossoms are usually pale blue, but sometimes they are white. The flower spikes are dense at first, becoming more extended as they mature. Though plants will bloom at a height of 6" or so, some plants get quite large, their spreading leaves and long stems radiating from the center.

High windswept ridges and stony alpine tundra are home for this wildflower. The fragrant lagotis blooms only at upper elevations, among the louseworts (*Pedicularis* spp.) and lichens.

It is interesting to note that while the species is widespread in Alaska and Asia, and reaches into the Aleutians from both directions, it has been recorded only in the eastern and western islands, not in the central Aleutians.

RANGE:
Widespread in Alaska and Asia.

Coastal Paintbrush, Honey Flower
Castilleja unalaschcensis (Cham. & Schlecht.) Malte

anisnaadam saaxaraa, aan-isnaadam saaxarangin or *qaatungin:* bumble-bee's sugar or favorite food

The stems arise from a hard, woody root and are upright and leafy, 8" to 24" tall. The leaves are alternate, long and lanceolate, ribbed, and often reddish green. The flowering top is a soft, tufted bundle of yellowish green, pubescent, rounded bracts. In the fall, the leaves and bracts disappear and the stems dry stiff. They bear at their top a cluster of hard, oval, two-celled capsules, which persist throughout the winter.

Coastal paintbrush is abundant in meadows and fields, often growing among cranesbill *(Geranium erianthum),* fleabane *(Erigeron peregrinus),* and ferns. Plucked from the center of the paintbrush, the innermost flowers have a sweet-tasting base, hence the local name honey flower or honeysuckle (although it is not in that family). The genus *Castilleja* is said to be partially parasitic on the roots of other plants (Anderson 1959).

RANGE:
Along the Pacific coast of Alaska, into the Aleutian and Pribilof Islands.

170

Eyebright
Euphrasia mollis (Ledeb.)
   Wettst.
(= *E. arctica* in part)

The single stems are thin and upright, pubescent, and often reddish, 1" to 5" tall. The leaves are small, up to ¾" long, with a few rounded teeth. The leaves are held in widely spaced opposite pairs along the stem and then bunched at the top with the flowers. The flowers are very small and inconspicuous, yellow or occasionally white, the tiny tubes opening into four lobes.

Eyebright looks something like a miniature version of the yellow rattle, the thin wiry stems holding a tiny cluster of flowers. It grows in wet areas with low vegetation, in meadows, and along lake shores.

RANGE:
Eastern Asia, throughout the Aleutians, and southwest coast of Alaska

Yellow Rattle, Rattlebox
Rhinanthus minor L.
   ssp. *borealis* (Stern.)
   A. Loeve
   (= *Rhinanthus minor* L. ssp.
   groenlandicus (Chab.)
   Neum, *R. groenlandicus*
   Chab., *R. crista-galli*
   Cham. & Schlecht.)

The single, slender stems are stiff and reddish green, usually less than 16" tall. The leaves are narrow and lanceolate, dentate, and held in opposite pairs. The bright yellow tubelike flowers are clustered among the top leaves, each emerging from a green, pocket-like calyx. In the fall, after the blossoms and leaves disappear, these calyxes turn delicate and papery. They are all that remain on the thin stems, rattling in the winds that shake out their flat, reddish brown seeds.

    The dry rattles remain intact through winter. Yellow rattle grows in grassy meadows and semidry areas.

RANGE:
Pacific coast and southwest Alaska, throughout the Aleutian Islands.

seed pods

Lousewort, Chamisso Lousewort, Bumblebee Flower
Pedicularis chamissonis
Steven

The Chamisso lousewort usually has a single stem, 8" to 24" tall. The leaves are long and fernlike, divided into narrow, finely toothed lobes, and they surround the upper stem in whorls of four. Both the leaves and the stems are glabrous. The flowers, held in a spike at the top, are light purple to lavender. The flower's tube bends at a right angle. The short upper lip ends in a beak which scarcely extends past the lower, three-cleft lip. The calyx, the pocket that holds the flower, is purple-striped.

A tall plant, the Chamisso lousewort is found in open meadows and fields, though not in abundance here. It is interesting to note that this is the only lousewort found throughout the Aleutians. It has come in from eastern Asia and is found in the Aleutian and Pribilof Islands and on the Alaska Peninsula, but nowhere else in Alaska (Hultén 1968). The other species found here are widespread in Alaska but reach only into the eastern Aleutian Islands.

RANGE:
Eastern Asia, Aleutian and Pribilof Islands, and on the Alaska Peninsula.

Lousewort, Langsdorf Lousewort
Pedicularis langsdorffii
Fisch.

Emerging from a stout tap-root, the stems are single, 1" to 7" tall. The leaves are long, narrow and fernlike, composed of many short toothed leaflets. The plants are sparsely woolly haired when young. The rose-pink to purple flowers are held in a short dense spike. The flower's two lips emerge from a slender tube. The lower lip is rounded and three-lobed, and the upper lip, or galea, is long, slender, and curving. In this species the galea bears a tiny but distinct sharp pair of teeth near the tip.

Louseworts are exquisite flowers with an unde-servedly odd name. The woolly lousewort, *Pedicularis lanata*, is very similar to this species, but lacks the teeth near the galea, and the plant has a very woolly flowering spike. Both louseworts are found only at upper elevations in the stony tundra of the high meadows and slopes.

RANGE:
Eastern Asia, the Arctic Coast, central Alaska and the Yukon, and the eastern Aleutians.

**Lousewort, Capitate
    Lousewort**
Pedicularis capitata
    J. Adams

The stems are stout and slightly pubescent, 1" to 5" tall. The basal leaves are long and fernlike, composed of numerous, small, lobed, and dissected leaflets. A pubescent, green, leaflike calyx holds the slender, tubular, and pale yellow flowers. The flowers are few and held in a short headlike, or capitate, cluster. The flowers have a long, curving upper lip, and the lower lip is three-cleft.

This lousewort is a short plant found on the tundra and rocky outcroppings of upper elevations. It often grows among lichens, bearberry (*Arctostaphylos* spp.), and other ericacious plants.

RANGE:
    Eastern Asia, the Arctic Coast, central Alaska and
    the Yukon, eastern Aleutians.

Woolly Lousewort
Pedicularis lanata Cham.
 & Schldl.
(= Pedicularis kanei
 Durand)

Emerging from a stout
taproot, the stems are
single, 6" to 8" tall. The
stems and flowering top
are densely woolly, and all
but the lower leaves are
covered when the plant
is young. The leaves are
long, narrow and fernlike,
composed of many short
toothed leaflets. The rose-
pink flowers are held in a
short dense spike. The two
lips of the flower emerge
from a slender tube. The lower lip is rounded
and has three lobes; the upper lip, or galea,
is long, slender and curving. In this species,
the galea is not toothed near the tip, distinguishing it from *Pedicularis langsdorffii.*
 It is found only at upper elevations on
the stony ridges and tundra.

RANGE:
Widespread across northern Canada and
Alaska, eastern Asia, into the eastern
Aleutians.

Bladderwort Family / *Lentibulariaceae*

Butterwort, Bog Violet
Pinguicula vulgaris L.

Emerging from fibrous roots, the flowering stems are reddish, slender, and leafless, 2" to 5" tall. The flattened, yellow green basal leaves are held close to the ground at the base of the stem, their edges curling inward. The leaves have a slippery, buttery feel and are used to trap and digest insects. The single flowers are violet, with five rounded lobes and a thin spur extending backwards from under the sepals.

A lovely and peculiar little flower, its common name of bog violet is misleading, since it is not a true violet *(Violaceae)*. The purple flower is similar, though; note the spur on the back of its corolla, a feature also seen on violets. Butterworts grow in wet meadows, bogs, and along stream banks, where the vegetation is low and mossy. Soil in this habitat is often acidic and nutrient poor, and the unusual adaption to digest and absorb insects enables the butterwort to take in nutrients from another source. This adaptation is a specialty of many bog plants, and butterworts are often found growing among sundews *(Drosera* spp.), another plant that captures insects.

Range:
Northern circumpolar, eastern and central Aleutians.

Plantain Family / *Plantaginaceae*

Seashore Plantain
Plantago macrocarpa
Cham. & Schlecht.

Emerging from a stout taproot, the plant forms leafy clusters to 16" tall. Long lanceolate leaves arise from the base of the plant. The leaves are glabrous, somewhat folded, with parallel veins. The numerous flowering stems are leafless, as long or longer than the leaves, each topped with a flowering spike to 2" or more long. Spikes are crowded with very small flowers with long conspicuous stamens. The fruits are oblong capsules.

A common and leafy plant, seashore plantain grows in wet meadows and along the beaches. The young, tender leaves can be gathered in the spring and eaten raw or steamed. The Unangan also used it medicinally; a tea made by boiling the roots was used as a tonic (Bank 1962).

RANGE:
Pacific coast of Alaska, Aleutian and Commander Islands.

Madder Family / *Rubiaceae*

Bedstraw, Cleavers
Galium aparine L.

Arising from taproots, the stems are squared, weak and branching, 12" to 60" long. The stems are often sprawling, forming loose extensive mats. The leaves are narrow and pointed, up to 2½" long and ⅛" wide and are held in whorls of six to eight. Both the stems and leaves are covered with fine bristles. The tiny white flowers with four petals are borne in the axils of the leaves. Bedstraw is a spindly, spreading beach plant that is springy underfoot, and burry to the touch. In late summer the plant bears small green fruits with hooked bristles that adhere to socks and sleeves.

fruits of the bedstraw

RANGE:
A northern circumpolar plant of the seashore, in Alaska it is found along the Pacific coast and throughout the Aleutians.

Sweet-Scented Bedstraw
Galium triflorum Michx.

Emerging from rhizomes, the stems are squared, weak and branching, and nearly glabrous. The stems are mostly upright or somewhat sprawling. The leaves are nearly glabrous, usually less than 2" long and up to ½" wide, and are held in whorls of six. The flowers are white and very tiny, borne on thin stalks arising from the axils of the leaves, and are almost always held in a set of three. The fruits are very small bristly balls, much smaller than the fruits of *G. aparine*.

As the name implies, this plant has a very sweet fragrance when it is dried. It has a somewhat more upright growing habit than *G. aparine,* and is much less bristly. It favors damp inland places, whereas *G. aparine* is strictly a coastal plant.

RANGE:
Northern circumpolar, southern Alaska, into the eastern Aleutians.

Other species:
Small bedstraw, *Galium trifidum* L., is also an inland plant but has smaller leaves than *G. triflorum,* which are mostly held in whorls of five or six. It usually bears its flowers singly or in pairs, on strongly curving pedicels, and its fruit is smooth, not bristly.

RANGE:
Small bedstraw is circumpolar and found throughout the Aleutians.

Honeysuckle Family / *Caprifoliaceae*

Twinflower
Linnaea borealis L.

Trailing along the ground, the stems are slender and rooting at the nodes, up to four feet long. The tiny evergreen leaves are leathery, oval to rounded, and held in opposite pairs. The thin flowering shoots stand upright, 2" to 3" tall, and fork at the top to hold a pair of fragrant, nodding pink bell-shaped flowers. In the fall, after the blossoms have dropped, the plants bear tiny, rounded sticky fruits, often found clinging to socks and pant legs.

Twinflower is a lovely and delicate ground cover, often growing on hillsides, twined among kinnikinnick *(Arctostaphylos urva-ursi)* and crowberry heath. *Linnaea borealis* is named for the Swedish botanist Karl von Linné (1707–1778). Linneaus, as his name is known in the Latin, is honored as the father of modern botany, having created the system of botanical nomenclature still used today.

RANGE:
Northern circumpolar; widespread across Alaska and throughout the Aleutians.

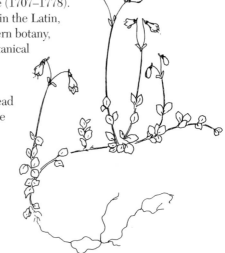

Bluebell Family / *Campanulaceae*

Bluebell, Harebell
Campanula chamissonis Fedorov
(= *C. dasyantha* Bieb.)

kulukulax̂ (from the Russian word for bell)

Emerging from a rhizome, the single flowering stem is 1" to 4" tall and often purplish. The basal leaves are held on short petioles and are elliptic to obovate and finely toothed. The stem leaves are sessile, smaller, and narrower. Flowering stems bear a single blue, bell-shaped flower.

The flower's tube opens into five long and pointed lobes, with soft white hairs along their margins. The sepals beneath are pubescent and blunt.

This lovely bluebell is found growing among the moss and crowberry heath of rocky ledges and stony tundra. It is similar to *C. lasiocarpa*, whose petals are more bluntly rounded and lacking the soft hairs. Both species of bluebells are found in only a few scattered locations, and plants are scarce. As with other uncommon plants, it is best not to pick them, but to enjoy them where they are.

RANGE:
Found only in Japan and the Aleutians.

Bluebell, Mountain Harebell
Campanula lasiocarpa Cham.

kulukulaˆx (from the Russian word for bell)

Emerging from a rhizome, the single flowering stem is 1" to 6" tall. The basal leaves are elliptic to oblong, with widely spaced teeth along their margins. The stem leaves are sessile, smaller, and narrower. The flowering stem bears a single, blue bell-shaped flower with a tube longer than the five broad lobes. The margins are glabrous (entirely lacking any hairs). The sepals beneath the flower are thin and pointed.

This bluebell is found scattered on rocky ledges and dry tundra.

RANGE:
Eastern Asia, throughout the Aleutians, and widespread across Alaska.

Other species:
Campanula uniflora L., a small harebell that is very rare in the eastern Aleutians, grows in similar habitats but is only 1" to 3" tall and bears tiny, semi-closed flowers.

Composite Family / *Asteraceae* or *Compositae*

Among the wildflowers in the Aleutians there are more species of *Compositae* than of any other family. They include our most familiar daisylike flowers like the fleabane *(Erigeron peregrinus)* and Siberian aster *(Aster sibiricus)*, and some of our medicinal plants such as yarrow *(Achillea borealis)*, artemisia *(Artemisia* spp.), and wild camomile *(Matricaria matricarioides)*.

The composites are the second largest family of flowering plants and are distributed worldwide. The first step toward identification of a plant in this large and complex family is to narrow it down to one of three groups. These groups are separated by the types of flowering heads. As the name composite implies, what we recognize as flowers are actually flowering heads composed of many individual flowers. These individual flowers come in two forms: ray flowers and disk flowers. Depending on the species at hand, the flowering heads may have: (1) both ray and disk flowers, (2) only ray flowers, or (3) only disk flowers. These three choices are the main dividing lines within the family. For example, the fleabane and Siberian aster, among others, are composed of both. What we commonly call the petals are the rays, or ligules, of the ray flowers which radiate from the central disk. The disk is composed of the many crowded tubular or disk flowers. Dandelions *(Taraxacum* spp.) and hawkweeds *(Hieracium* spp.) have only ray flowers and lack a central disk. Artemisia *(Artemisia* spp.) and pearly everlasting *(Anaphalis margaritacea)* have only disk flowers, although the surrounding bracts sometimes look like rays.

To narrow a plant down further to its genus, look for other distinctions such as the color of the rays, whether the flowering heads are solitary or many, and whether the leaves are opposite or alternate, divided or simple. Identification at the species level sometimes requires a hand lens, a keen knowledge of the flower's parts, and a new vocabulary of descriptive terms. This is the best way to learn the identification of these plants but requires time and patience.

While more than two dozen species of *Compositae* have been recorded in the islands, not all of them extend throughout the chain. Asters are found only in the eastern islands. Arctic daisies *(Chrysanthemum arcticum)* grow in the western and central islands, and the Kamchatka thistle *(Cirsium kamtschaticum)* has been recorded only in the westernmost Aleutian Islands.

184

Goldenrod, Northern Goldenrod
Solidago multiradiata Ait.

Emerging from a short woody rhizome, the stems are stiff and reddish. Plants may grow to 20" tall, but are more often dwarfed. The leaves are oblong to lanceolate, alternate, the margins entire or remotely toothed. The leaves become smaller toward the top of the stem, and rarely extend past the flowering top.

The small yellow flowering heads are held in a dense rounded cluster, and the flower's rays are less than ¼" long.

Goldenrod grows in meadows as well as rocky soil, and is often found along roadsides.

RANGE:
Widespread in northern North America including Alaska and throughout the Aleutians.

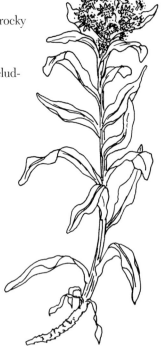

Siberian Aster
Aster sibiricus L.

Emerging from elongate rhizomes, the stems are 4" to 16" tall. Highly variable, the stems may be tall and branching into many heads, or shorter with a single head and stem. The stems and leaves are glabrous to sparsely covered with soft hairs beneath. The leaves are alternate, lanceolate, the margins varying from slightly serrated to entire. The flowering heads have narrow, pointed, bluish purple rays surrounding the yellow central disks.

A September companion, the Siberian aster shares in the bittersweet brilliance of fall. The species is often difficult to distinguish from *Aster subspicatus*, and both plants are highly variable. Generally, *Aster subspicatus* is taller, with stems 12" to 36" tall, again either single or branching. But separating the two also requires a look at the phyllaries, or involucral bracts. These are the narrow leaf-like parts that are held in a whorl under the flowering head. In *Aster sibiricus*, these bracts are pubescent on the back; in *Aster subspicatus* they are glabrous on the back but ciliate on their margins.

—*continues*

The fleabane *(Erigeron peregrinus)*, another similar species, is an earlier bloomer, and compared with its pink and frilly head, the *Aster sibiricus'* rays are fewer and a deeper luminous blue purple.

   Both species of asters are common and conspicuous when blooming in the fall, often growing in patches on hillsides, in grassy meadows and fields, and along riverbanks.

RANGE:
Aster sibiricus: Nearly circumpolar and widespread across Alaska, but only reaching into the eastern Aleutians.

RANGE:
Aster subspicatus: Along the Pacific Coast and into the eastern Aleutians.

Aster subspicatus

Composite Family / Asteraceae or Compositae

Fleabane, Coastal Fleabane
Erigeron peregrinus
(Pursh) Greene
(= *Aster peregrinus* Pursh)

Arising from an elongated, woody rhizome, the stems are single, often gently bending, and 8" to 20" tall. The stems are pubescent. The leaves are soft and numerous, alternate, oblong to lanceolate, the margins bearing fine hairs.

The flowering heads are single; the ray flowers are many and overlapping, varying in color from pale purple and pink to almost white, surrounding a yellow central disk.

Fleabane is abundant in Unalaska's meadows and hillsides. Local residents often refer to it as a daisy. It blooms in midsummer, earlier than the asters.

RANGE:
Along the Pacific coast of Alaska, the Aleutians and Commander Islands of Russia.

Left: Very scarce but found at high elevations is the low-growing arctic daisy, Erigeron humilis *Graham* (= E. unalaskensis *(DC.) Ledeb.)*

Composite Family / Asteraceae or Compositae

Pussytoes, Single-headed Pussytoes
Antennaria monocephala DC.

The plant forms low-growing mats, with upright flowering stems 1" to 4"
tall. The leaves are less than ½" long, the upper surface green and sometimes glabrous, the under surface grayish and pubescent. The basal leaves
are spatulate to spoon-shaped, tipped with a short,
abrupt point, and the leaf edges often curl inwards.
The flowering stem leaves are narrower and linear in shape. Each stem bears a solitary
flowering head, less than ½" across.
The heads are round and flattened,
white and papery, later turning
brown and dry. The styles are long and
conspicuous, extending above the flowers. The phyllaries (or outer involucral
bracts) which surround the inner
bracts of the flower, are dark brown
to black to greenish black.
    The flowering heads of this pussytoes
look like small white buttons. This *single* head distin-
guishes it from the other *Antennaria* species, which all
bear numerous flowering heads on each stem. The plant grows
in dry stony tundra and is often found at upper elevations or along the
roadsides where the vegetation is low.

RANGE:
Widespread across Alaska and into the Aleutian Islands.

Pussytoes, Pink Pussytoes
Antennaria rosea E. L. Greene

These plants form low-growing mats, with upright flowering stems to 6" tall. The leaves are light grayish green and tomentose on both surfaces. The basal leaves are spatulate to oblanceolate, up to ¾" long and tipped with a short, abrupt point. The flowering stem leaves are narrower and linear in shape and up to 1" long. Each stem bears a cluster of flowering heads, from three to twelve or more, and the whole cluster is about ¾" across. The heads are small and papery, whitish at their centers, turning brown with age. The phyllaries (or outer involucral bracts) that surround the inner bracts of the flower are rosy to pinkish.

These pussytoes look like tiny, pinkish pearly everlastings (*Anaphalis margaritacea*). They favor dry stony tundra or rocky cliffs and sometimes grow along old roadsides. They can be found at upper elevations as well as near sea level.

The pinkish phyllaries and numerous flowering heads distinguish this species from the single-headed pussytoes, *A. monocephala*. Another multi-headed species that has been identified from Unalaska is the alpine pussytoes, *A. alpina* (L.) Gaertner [UAF Herbarium]. It usually has fewer heads and shorter stems, and the phyllaries are black to greenish black. Members of this genus can be difficult to identify at the species level. For a number of species, male plants are absent or rare in some areas, and the female flowers are able to produce seeds asexually, creating genetically identical offspring.

RANGE:
Widespread across North America and Alaska.

Pearly Everlasting
Anaphalis margaritacea (L.)
Benth. & Hook.

(A) *kamgii quhmax̂,
kamgingis quhmas:* its
head is white.

Ascending from long
creeping rhizomes, the
stems are leafy and un-
branched, 8" to 24" tall.
The leaves are soft and
narrowly lanceolate, green
and glabrous above, pale
and tomentose underneath.
The small, papery white
flowering heads are nu-
merous, forming a round
cluster.

The heads lack ray flowers; the central disk
is surrounded by narrow pearly white bracts.

Pearly everlasting is a late summer
favorite of the meadows and hillsides. It
grows in stands and is easily recognized
by its felt-like stems and leaves and the
papery clusters of small white flowers. If
the flowers are picked before the centers
turn brown and the seed loosens, pearly
everlastings dry and keep quite well, as
the name implies. For winter bouquets
it is best to hang them upside down until
the stems dry straight.

Range:
Widespread across North America;
in Alaska, along the Pacific coast,
throughout the Aleutians, and eastern
Asia.

Yarrow
Achillea borealis Bong.

(E) *ulngiĝdagax̂,
uulngiiĝdigax̂.
chngaatuudax̂* from the
root word *chngax̂:* hair,
fur, pelt
(A) *saahmikaadax̂,
saamikaadax̂, samikayax̂*

Emerging from a slender
rhizome, the stems are
upright, 8" to 20" tall, fibrous, and covered with
long hairs. The deeply aromatic leaves are long and
pinnate; the tiny leaflets
are finely divided and held
along opposite sides of the
stem. The flowering heads form flat dense clusters; the rays are usually
white, but sometimes pinkish.

Yarrow is a common and hardy plant with
strongly scented, lacy green leaves. Rubbed
in the hands and breathed in, they are the
scent of summer. The plant grows in dry areas,
in sandy or rocky soil, from sea level to upper
elevations. The flowers bloom late into the fall.
Worldwide, yarrow has long been known
for its medicinal qualities, and the
Unangan used it for such purposes
as well. Its crushed leaves act as a
coagulant, and when held to a wound or
cut will stem the bleeding. A tea steeped from the
leaves will reduce fever and help relieve chest colds
and stomach pains. Gargling a warm tea soothes a
sore throat. Also, the yarrow's root is said to have
anesthetic properties (Schofield 1989).

RANGE:
Widespread across North America and Alaska,
throughout the Aleutians.

Pineapple Weed, Wild Camomile
Matricaria matricarioides (Less.) Porter
(= *M. suaveolens* (Pursh) Buch.)

ramaaskaᵃ̂x, from the Russian *romashka*

Arising from fibrous taproots, the stems are glabrous, branching and often curving from the base, and are seldom more than 8" high. The leaves are bright green and finely divided into very narrow segments. The plants bear numerous, yellow, conical, heads.

Wild camomile is a hardy little aromatic plant that grows in small clumps in poor or rocky soil. I only half-jokingly call it a parking lot plant, because it thrives in dry disturbed gravel where most other plants do not grow, and people really are apt to find it growing under their trucks. Wild camomile, like the cultivated species, can be brewed to make a soothing tea. The Unangan, and Russians as well, used it medicinally, and the tea was said to be a good tonic and a laxative (Bank 1962).

RANGE:
Northern circumpolar and widespread across Alaska; scattered populations in the Aleutians.

Artemisia, Wormwood
Artemisia unalaskensis
Rybd.

sixsiqax̂

Arising from a stout rootstock, the stems are fibrous and very leafy, to 40" tall. The leaves are aromatic, deeply cleft into long lobes, silvery green, and tomentose underneath. The top of the plant narrows into a tassel of small, inconspicuous greenish purple flowers, which are bunched among the leaves.

A hardy plant, often shoulder high, this artemisia grows in stands from sea level upwards. The leaves have a wonderful, strong scent, and were widely used medicinally by Alaska Native peoples. In traditional Unangan steam-baths, the leafy stems are gently slapped against the skin. The steamed leaves can be used as a hot pack to relieve aches and pains. A tea steeped from the leaves can ease colds, sore throats, and stomachaches (Schofield 1989).

RANGE:
Japan, Kamchatka, and the Aleutians.

A. unalaskensis is closely related to *A. tilesii*, a similar wormwood that is highly variable in its morphology. Hultén (1968) describes four subspecies for this circumpolar group, and it is often difficult to distinguish among these subspecies, all of which could also be found in the Aleutians.

Arctic Wormwood
Artemisia arctica Less.

Emerging from a stout, woody taproot, the stems are glabrous and reddish, 8" to 24" tall. The bright green leaves are finely divided and clustered near the base of the plant, thinning to almost lacking on the upper stems. The numerous small, flowering heads are nodding and loosely clustered along the upper stem. The tiny rays are yellowish.

Usually found at upper elevations, arctic wormwood grows in scattered areas of dry tundra among the ericacious plants. Unlike *A. unalaskensis*, the finely cut leaves are not fragrant.

RANGE:
Widespread across eastern Asia and Alaska, lacking in the central Aleutians.

Sweet Coltsfoot
Petasites frigidus (L.)
Franchet

Arising from stout creeping rhizomes, the flowering stems are simple and up to 20" tall. The flowering stems develop before the basal leaves do, emerging separately from them along the rhizome. The basal leaves are held on long petioles and are heart-shaped to triangular, shallowly lobed, and coarsely toothed. Their upper surface is nearly glabrous and dark green, the under surface whitish and tomentose (covered in short wooly hairs). The flowering stem bears alternate reddish bracts and a flat-topped cluster of flowering heads. The flowers are white to pinkish, small, and very fragrant.

Sweet coltsfoot is uncommon on Unalaska Island and populations are scattered. The plants are found at upper elevations where the vegetation is low, and in areas of wet tundra and drainage slopes.

RANGE:
Widespread across Alaska, the Yukon, and Eurasia, with scattered populations in the eastern and central Aleutians.

Unalaska Arnica
Arnica unalaschcensis Less.

The stems are green, unbranching, 4" to 12" tall, and pubescent (covered in short, soft hairs). The leaves, held in three to five pairs, are bluntly lanceolate, ribbed, and pubescent. The flowering heads are always single. The bright yellow rays are distinctly notched at the ends. The tiny anthers surrounding the center are purple.

Unalaska arnica is a bright little bloom of upper elevations, stony tundra and rocky outcroppings. It is often found growing among louseworts (*Pedicularis* spp.) and lichens. The similar *Arnica chamissonis* is usually taller and often has numerous flowering heads.

RANGE:
Japan, Kamchatka, Aleutians, and Bering Sea islands.

Arnica
Arnica chamissonis Less.

The stems are slender, 8" to 32" tall and often reddish near the base. Both the stems and leaves are pubescent (covered in short, soft hairs). The leaves are held in four to ten pairs along the stem, lanceolate, and sometimes shallowly toothed. The flowering heads are sometimes single but more often numerous. The rays are bright yellow and shallowly notched at the ends, the anthers are also yellow. The flowering heads tend to tilt sideways.

These arnicas bloom in mid to late summer and are common in fields and meadows. They often grow in patches.

RANGE:
Across western North America; southeast and southwest Alaska, into the eastern Aleutians.

Seabeach Senecio, Ragwort, Seashore Sunflower
Senecio pseudo-arnica
    Less.

(E) *alngaayux̂*
(A) *uxchuudax̂,
    uxchuĝaadax̂*

Stems are stout, very leafy and often curving, to 40" tall. The leaves are large and fleshy, to 10" long or more. The upper surface of the leaves is glabrous and dark green and the under surface is tomentose (covered in short wooly hairs).
        The leaves are oblong to broadly lanceolate, with small, widely spaced teeth. The sunny yellow flowering heads, often solitary or few, are 3" to 5" across; the bright yellow rays surrounding a dense, darker yellow center. By fall the tufted seeds at the center have ripened and are carried off by the winds.

Seabeach senecio is a hardy coastal plant. Salt tolerant, it thrives along sand or gravel shores among the grasses and beach greens *(Honckenya peploides)*. An Unangan medicinal practice was to gather the leaves when the plant was in bloom, and tie them over sores to help them heal (Bank 1962).

RANGE:
Widespread along the Pacific and Bering Sea coasts of Alaska, throughout the Aleutians and eastern Asia.

Dandelions
Taraxacum spp.

Emerging from taproots, the flowering stems are slender, leafless and hollow, containing a milky juice. The leaves are all basal, forming a rosette on the ground. The leaves are glabrous, long and spatulate, the margins varying from deeply lobed to subentire. Each stem bears a single, bright yellow flowering head. Dandelions are composed only of ray flowers and have no central disk. The flowering heads later form downy orbs of parachuting seeds.

Dandelions are a difficult group and are best considered at the genus level. Their unusual breeding system allows them to form viable seeds without fertilization. In this way, local races or microspecies of exactly similar plants are produced.

Dandelions grow in moist places, often in poor soil and disturbed areas. The leaves make tasty greens and are less apt to be bitter if picked before the plant blooms. The root is also good tasting, once peeled of its brown skin and steamed or added to salads; the only hard part is digging them up.

RANGE:
As a genus, found throughout Alaska and spread or introduced throughout much of the world.

FOUND IN THE ALEUTIANS:
Taraxacum ceratophorum (Ledeb.) DC.
    T. kamtschaticum Dahlstedt
    T. officinale Weber
    T. trigonolobum Dahlstedt

Rattlesnake Root
Prenanthes alata (Hook.)
   Dietr.
(= *P. lessingii* Hult.)

Plants emerge from a long and slender taproot. In its early stage, the plant sends up only the large low-growing leaves; later the slender flowering stems arise 8" to 16" tall. The leaves are glabrous and irregularly toothed. The lower leaves are the largest, held on winged petioles, and are hastate (arrowhead shaped), the basal lobes pointing back or outwards. Up the stem the leaves become progressively shorter petioled and triangular, the uppermost nearly sessile and diamond shaped. The flowering heads are held in a loose and somewhat nodding cluster at the top of the stem, and emerging from the axils of the uppermost leaves. The flowering heads are less than an inch across, the ray flowers are white and finely notched at the tips, the long styles extending beyond them. The seeds at the center are attached to soft reddish brown bristles. The unopened buds are elongate, enclosed in their dark green, lanceolate bracts.

Rattlesnake root is very uncommon here where it is near the western end of its range. The white flowers are very pretty, but the distinctive leaves will more likely catch your attention. The plant blooms in mid- to late summer in its habitat of dry open slopes and cliffs, along streams and in rocky soil.

RANGE:
U.S. Pacific Northwest coast out to the eastern Aleutians.

Hawkweed, Woolly Hawkweed
Hieracium triste Willd.

Arising from woody, fibrous roots, the flowering stems are thin and nearly leafless and 4" to 12" tall. The basal leaves are oblong to lanceolate, tapering to short petioles. The flowering stems bear a few reduced leaves. The upper stem and flowering heads are densely covered with dark gray hairs. The few to several flowering heads are small and often somewhat closed, with bright yellow rays.
The hawkweed's flowers look like small and very woolly dandelions. Rather uncommon here, it grows in scattered locations of dry tundra heath or stony slopes, most often at upper elevations.

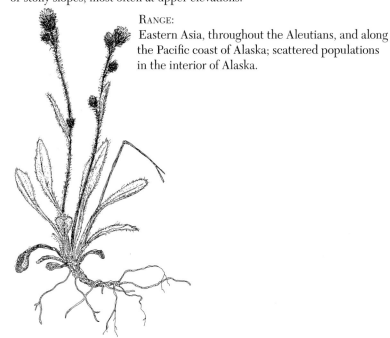

RANGE:
Eastern Asia, throughout the Aleutians, and along the Pacific coast of Alaska; scattered populations in the interior of Alaska.

Composite Family / *Asteraceae or Compositae*

References

Anderson, J. P. 1959. *Flora of Alaska and Adjacent Parts of Canada*. Ames: Iowa State University Press.

Bank, Theodore P., II. 1952. *Botanical and Ethnobotanical Studies in the Aleutian Islands*. Reprinted from Papers of the Michigan Academy of Science, Arts and Letters, vol. 37. p.13–30. 1951. Ann Arbor: University of Michigan.

————. 1962. *Medicinal Plant Lore of the Aleut*. The Proceedings of the Ninth Pacific Science Congress, 1957, vol. 4, 1962. p. 281–284. Ann Arbor: University of Michigan.

Bergsland, Knut, comp. 1994. *Aleut Dictionary. Unangam Tunudgusii*. Fairbanks: Alaska Native Language Center, University of Alaska Fairbanks.

Collet, Dominique. 1996. *Willows of the Kenai Peninsula*. Kenai, Alaska: The Kenai Peninsula Botanical Society.

Drewes, Harald, G. D. Fraser, G. L. Snyder and H. F. Barnett, Jr. 1961. *Geology of Unalaska Island and Adjacent Insular Shelf, Aleutian Islands, Alaska*. Geological Survey Bulletin 1028-S. Washington, D.C.: United States Government Printing Office.

Dumond, Don E., and Richard A. Knecht. 2001. An Early Blade Site in the Eastern Aleutians. In *Archaeology in the Aleut Zone of Alaska*. University of Oregon Anthropological Papers 58.

Graham, Frances Kelso, and the Ouzinkie Botanical Society. 1985. *Plantlore of an Alaskan Island*. Anchorage: Alaska Northwest Publishing Company.

Hamilton, Thomas D., and Robert M. Thorson. 1986. Glacial Geology of the Aleutian Islands. Based on the Contributions of Robert F. Black. In *Glaciation in Alaska. The Geologic Record*. Anchorage: Alaska Geological Society.

Harrington, H. D., and L. W. Durrell. 1981. *How to Identify Plants*. Athens, Ohio: Ohio University Press.

Harris, James G., and Melinda Woolf Harris. 1994. *Plant Identification Terminology: An Illustrated Glossary*. Spring Lake, Utah: Spring Lake Publishing Company

Haskin, Leslie L. 1977. *Wild Flowers of the Pacific Coast*. New York: Dover Publications, Inc.

Heller, C. A. 1966. *Wild, Edible and Poisonous Plants of Alaska*. Fairbanks: University of Alaska Cooperative Extension Service.

Hopkins, David M., ed. 1967. *The Bering Land Bridge*. Stanford, California: Stanford University Press.

Hudson, Ray, ed. 1977. *Cuttlefish One*. Unalaska, Alaska: Unalaska City School.

———. 1992. *Unugulux Tunusangin: Oldtime Stories.* Unalaska, Alaska: Unalaska City School District.

Hudson, Ray, and Ismael Gromoff, eds. 1975. *Aleut for Beginners.* Unalaska, Alaska: Unalaska City School.

Hultén, Eric. 1960. *Flora of the Aleutian Islands,* 2d ed. New York: J. Cramer, Hafner Publishing Company.

———. 1968. *Flora of Alaska and Neighboring Territories.* Stanford, California: Stanford University Press.

Jochelson, Waldemar. 1933. *History, Ethnology and Anthropology of the Aleut.* Washington D.C.: Carnegie Institution.

Jones, Anore. 1981. Plants and Trees. *The Kotzebue Basin.* Alaska Geographic vol. 8, no. 3. Anchorage: The Alaska Geographic Society.

Laughlin, William S. 1980. *Aleuts: Survivors of the Bering Land Bridge.* Austin, Texas: Holt, Rinehart and Winston.

Luer, C. A. 1975. *The Native Orchids of the U.S. and Canada.* New York: New York Botanical Garden.

MacKinnon, Andy, Jim Pojar, and Ray Coupé, eds. 1992. *Plants of Northern British Columbia.* Edmonton, Alberta: Lone Pine Publishing.

Mann, Daniel H., and Thomas D. Hamilton. 1995. Late Pleistocene and Holocene Paleoenvironments of the North Pacific Coast. Quaternary Science Reviews, vol. 14, no. 5, p. 449–471.

Morgan, Lael, ed. 1980. *The Aleutians.* Alaska Geographic vol. 7, no. 3. Anchorage: The Alaska Geographic Society.

Pielou, E. C. 1991. *After the Ice Age.* Chicago: University of Chicago Press.

———. 1994. *A Naturalist's Guide to the Arctic.* Chicago: University of Chicago Press.

Raven, Peter H., Ray F. Evert, and Susan E. Eichhorn. 1992. *Biology of Plants.* New York: Worth Publishers.

Rennick, Penny, ed. 1994. *The Alaska Peninsula.* Alaska Geographic vol. 21, no. 1. Anchorage: The Alaska Geographic Society.

———. 1994. *Prehistoric Alaska.* Alaska Geographic vol. 21, no. 4. Anchorage: The Alaska Geographic Society.

Saville, D. B. O. 1972. *Arctic Adaptations in Plants.* Monograph No. 6. Ottawa: Canada Dept. of Agriculture.

Schofield, Janice, J. 1989. *Discovering Wild Plants.* Anchorage: Alaska Northwest Books.

Trelawny, John G. 1988. *Wildflowers of the Yukon, Alaska, and Northwestern Canada.* Victoria, BC: Sono Nis Press.

van Schaak, George B. 1945. *Flowers of Island X.* Unpublished mss. Welfare and Recreation Department. Navy 163. U.S.A.

Veniaminov, Ivan. 1984. *Notes on the Islands of the Unalashka District.* Fairbanks, Alaska: Limestone Press.

Viereck, Eleanor G. 1987. *Alaska Wilderness Medicines.* Anchorage: Alaska Northwest Publishing Company.

Viereck, Leslie A., and Elbert L. Little, Jr. 1972. *Alaska Trees and Shrubs.* Agriculture Handbook No. 410. Washington, D.C.: U.S.D.A. Forest Service.

Welsh, Stanley L. 1974. *Anderson's Flora of Alaska and Adjacent Parts of Canada*. Provo, Utah: Brigham Young University Press.

White, Helen A., and Maxcine Williams, eds. 1974. *The Alaska-Yukon Wildflowers Guide*. Anchorage: Alaska Northwest Publishing Company.

Zwinger, Ann H., and Beatrice E. Willard. 1972. *Land Above The Trees. A Guide to American Alpine Tundra*. Tucson: The University of Arizona Press.

Pronunciation Guide

The pronunciation and use of Unangax̂ words takes some practice but is encouraged. Most of the letters are pronounced as they are in English. Only a few sounds in the language have no English equivalents. Some of them may seem difficult at first, but it is mostly a matter of learning to form the sounds.
The vowels are in two forms: short and long. The long vowels are held open for a longer period.

Both *a* and *aa* sound like the English *a*, as in father; the *aa* is held open longer.

i sounds like the English *i*, as in hit or is.

ii sounds like the English *ee*, as in meet.

u is like the *u* in pull.

uu is like the *oo* in tool.

Most of the consonants are pronounced as they are in English, with the following exceptions:

d sounds like the English *th*, as in mother.

g (a voiced velar fricative) is softer than the English *g*. It is made in the same position but with the tongue held differently. The back of the tongue is raised toward, but not touching, the soft part of the roof of the mouth. It does not make contact or stop the air as the English g does.

x (a voiceless velar fricative) is similar to the Aleut g above but the tongue is lowered slightly and the breath is released voicelessly, as when pronouncing the English h.

ĝ (a voiced uvular fricative) is made with the back of the tongue held against the soft palate, where the uvula is, from the spot where one would gargle. The sound is made with friction.

x̂ (voiceless uvular fricative) is similar to *ĝ* but the breath is released voicelessly, like an English *h* but from way back in the throat.

q (a voiceless uvular stop) is like a hard English *k* made way back in the throat, nearly where one would clear it. The breath is stopped and then sharply released with the back of the tongue.

ng always sounds like the English *ng* as in singer, never as *ng* plus *g* as in the word finger.

208

This is not a complete guide but is intended to help with beginning pronunciation. While some Unangan plant names are still everyday household words, others are at risk of being forgotten. Perhaps the repetition of these names will help to keep the knowledge of them alive. Please see the Introduction for more on Unangan names and traditional uses for plants.

Pronunciation Guide

Index to Aleut or Unangan Names for Plants

Words from the Eastern dialect are indicated with (E), those from the Atkan dialect with (A), and those from the Attu dialect with (Attu).

Index to Botanical Names

Index to Botanical Names

Index to Botanical Names

Index to Common Names

aconite, Kamchatka, 74–75
adder's mouth, 39
adder's tongue, white, 39
alder, 53
anemone, narcissis-flowered 77
anemone, yellow, 76
angelica, seacoast, 131–132
arnica, 196,197
arnica, Unalaska 196
artemisia, 193,194
asphodel, northern, 20
asphodel, Scotch, 21
asters, 185–186
aster, Siberian, 185–186
avens, 110–112
avens, large-leaved, 110
avens, low, 112
avens, Ross, 112
azalea, alpine 142

beach greens, 67
beach lovage, 128–129
bearberry, 146
bearberry, alpine 147–148
bedstraw, 178,179
bedstraw, small, 179
bedstraw, sweet-scented, 179
Birch family, 53
bistort, alpine 60
bittercress, see cress
blackberry, 139–140
Bladderwort family, 176
bluebells, 181–182
Bluebell family, 181–182
blueberries, 150–152
blueberry, lowbush, 152
blueberry, highbush, 150–151
bog candles, 31
bog orchids, 30–34
bog violet, 176
Borage family, 160
brooklime, 164
Buckwheat family, 54–60
bumblebee flower, 162, 172
bunchberry, 135–136
burnet, Sitka great 113
buttercups, 78–84

buttercup, Bongard, 83–84
buttercup, common, 82
buttercup, creeping, 81
buttercup, Eschscholtz 80
Buttercup family, 70–85
buttercup, snowbed, 80
butterwort, 176

camomile, wild, 192
celery, wild, 133–134
chickweeds, 63–65
chickweed, Bering, 64
Chickweed family, 63–69
chickweed, mouse-ear, 65
cinquefoil, 106, 107
cinquefoil, marsh or purple, 106
cleavers, 178
cliff hanger, 91
coltsfoot, sweet, 195
Composite family, 183–201
coral-root, early, 38
cornel, Canadian dwarf, 136
cornel, Swedish or Lapland, 135–136
cornflower, 30
cotton flower, 18, 19
cotton grass, 18, 19
cotton grass, russett 19
cow parsnip, 133–134
cowslip, 70–71
cranberry, bog, 153
cranberry, mountain, 149
cranesbill, 118–119
cress, 88–93
cress, hairy rock, 93
cress, Kamchatka rock, 92
cress, northern rock, 90
cress, umbel-flowered bitter, 89
cress, winter, 88
crowberry, 139–140
Crowberry family, 139–140
Crowfoot family, 70–85
crowfoot, white water, 78
cucumber, wild, 24

daisy, arctic, 187
dandelions, 199
docks, 57–58

215

plantain, seashore, 177
poppy, Alaska, 85
Poppy family, 85
primrose, Chukchi, 154
Primrose family, 154–156
primrose, Greenland, 155
primrose, wedge-leaved, 155
ptarmigan grass, 60
Purslane family, 61–62
pussytoes, 188–189
pussytoes, pink, 189
pussytoes, single-headed, 188
putchki, 133–134
putchki, St. Paul, 131–132
pyrola, 137, 138

ragwort, 298
rainflower, 61–62, 83–84
rattlebox, 171
rattlesnake root, 200
rhododendron, Kamchatka, 143
rhubarbs, wild, 57–58
rice root, 22
river beauty, 123
rock cress, see cress
Rose family, 102–113

salmonberry, 104
sandwort, blunt-leaved, 68
sandwort, grove 68
sandwort, seabeach, 67
sarana lily, 22
saxifrage, bracted, 99
saxifrage, brook, 98
saxifrage, cordate-leaved, 95
saxifrage, thyme-leaved, 95
Saxifrage family, 95–101
saxifrage, leather-leaved, 95, 96
saxifrage, purple mountain, 97
saxifrage, tufted, 100
scurvy weed, 67, 87
sea lovage, 128–129
sea lungwort, 160
seashore sunflower, 198
Sedge family, 18–19
self-heal, 161
senecio, seabeach, 198
shooting star, 153
shrub willows, 48–52
sibbaldia, 109
Siberian spring beauty, 61–62
sidebells wintergreen, 138
silverweed, pacific, 108
single-sided pyrola, 138
sorrel, alpine or mountain, 59

sorrel, garden or green 56
sorrel, sheep 55
sorrels, 55–56, 59
sourgrass, 59
spearwort, creeping, 79
speedwells, 165–167
speedwell, Aleutian 167
speedwell, alpine 165
speedwell, low, 166
speedwell, Steller, 167
speedwell, thyme-leaved, 166
spoonwort, 87
starflower, arctic 156
starwort, northern, 63
starwort, ruscus-leave, 62, 63
starwort, Sitka, 63
stinky flower, 22
strawberry, beach or wild, 105
Sundew family, 94
sundew, round-leaved 94

thrift, v
thyme-leaved saxifrage, 95
twayblade, broad-leaved, 36
twayblade, heart-leaved, 37
twinflower, 180
twisted stalk, 24

veronicas, 164–167
vetch, 116
vetchling, 117
violet, Alaska, 120
violet, bog, 176
Violet family, 120

Waterleaf family, 159
watermelon berry, 24
Water Milfoil family, 127
weasel snout, 168
white flower, 77
white water crowfoot, 78
wild camomile, 192
wild celery, 133–134
wild cucumber, 24
wild flag, 25
wild geranium, 118–119
wild iris, 25
wild pea, 117
wild rhubarbs, 57–58
wild strawberry, 105
wild sweet potato, 108
willow, Alaska, 50
willow, arctic or ground, 47
willow, Barclay, 52
willows, dwarf, 42–47

217

Index to Common Names

Suzi Golodoff, a long-time Unalaska resident, reflects her love for her island home in this lovely and useful guide. She has been a salmon fisherman, artist, and naturalist in the Aleutians, and enjoys spending time at the remote cabin she and her husband built on Unalaska Island.